Maps are often based on older maps. But have you ever wondered who makes new *maps—and how they go about it?*

Today's mapmakers start with stereo photographs taken from specially equipped planes. Yet this is just the beginning. As you will read in this book, dozens of specialists (including rugged engineers who scale mountain peaks) work for two years to prepare one new map of a small area.

Illustrated with unusual maps and photographs, All About Maps and Mapmaking *tells the fascinating story behind U.S. government maps, road maps, charts for the jet age—and even maps of proposed landing sites on the moon.*

All About

MAPS AND MAPMAKING

allabout
books

random house: new york

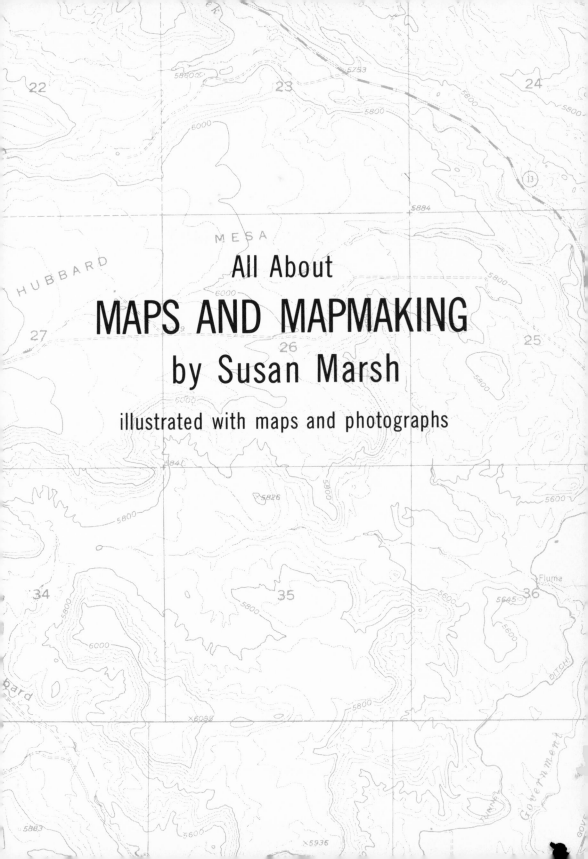

All About
MAPS AND MAPMAKING
by Susan Marsh

illustrated with maps and photographs

For help in the preparation of this book, the author and the publisher wish to thank Gerard L. Alexander, Chief of the Map Division, New York Public Library.

For technical information and assistance, grateful acknowledgment is due to Thomas V. Cummins, Topographic Engineer, U.S. Geological Survey, Denver; David A. Day, Dean of Engineering, University of Denver; Gerald FitzGerald, retired Chief Topographic Engineer, U.S. Geological Survey; Lt. Col. Edward F. Franke and Lt. Col. Thomas W. Whitchurch, U.S. Army Map Service; Frances Rizzari, head of reproduction, U.S. Geological Survey, Denver; Albert A. Stanley, Special Assistant to the Director, U.S. Coast and Geodetic Survey; and John I. White, Vice President, General Drafting Company.

The following also furnished helpful advice: Dr. Prudence Bostwick, past president, Association for Supervision and Curriculum Development; Mary Lee Keath, past president, American Association of School Librarians; and Dr. Kenneth Oberholtzer, past president, American Association of School Administrators.

Illustration credits: Alice Marsh Abbott, page 5 (top); Canadian Department of Mines and Technical Surveys, 87; Cubic Corporation, 31; General Drafting Company, 6, 75, 77; Susan Marsh and Elmer Smith, 84–85; Minneapolis-Honeywell Regulator Company, 137; Elmer Smith, 14, 17, 26, 36; U.S. Air Force (Aeronautical Chart and Information Center), 111, 126; U.S. Army Map Service, 123, 135; U.S. Coast and Geodetic Survey, 7, 89, 91, 95, 96, 98, 102, 107, 110, 112, 113; U.S. Geological Survey, 5 (bottom), 11, 15, 19, 20, 34, 35, 42, 46, 47, 51, 55, 60, 62, 64, 66, 68, 72, 118, 119, 130, 133, title page, and end papers.

Designed by JANE BYERS

Library of Congress catalog card number: 63-7825

Contents

All About

MAPS AND MAPMAKING

Maps
and Map Readers

A few years ago, maps played an important part in the greatest rescue operation of United States history.

Hurricane Carla was approaching the Gulf States. The U.S. Weather Bureau predicted that the Gulf of Mexico would rise 18 feet above normal at the eye of the hurricane—and that it would flood inland for many miles.

How many miles? The Red Cross and the Texas Department of Public Safety urgently needed to know.

A map expert told them exactly. He studied hundreds of government maps that showed the exact height of the land above sea level. Near the predicted eye of the hurricane, he found where the ground is 20 feet above normal high water. As a result of his warnings nearly 300,000 people left their homes for high ground —and safety.

DIFFERENT MAPS FOR DIFFERENT PURPOSES

We all have maps in our heads. One of these private maps tells where the sun rises and sets. Other maps show where friends live, or how to get to the grocery store.

It is difficult to transfer the map from one person's head to another. When the route is too complicated for pointing, or for words, a written map helps.

On the next page is a homemade map to help guests find their way to a mountain cabin. Although it is not accurate, it is a very good map—for it does what it is supposed to do. It shows how to make the proper turns where the nameless roads fork. It points out landmarks to watch for.

The homemade map was designed for one special use. Probably it was thrown away afterward. But most maps have to serve many different uses. They include more facts than any one person needs for a single purpose. An accurate map of the same area as the homemade map shows the house where the party was held,

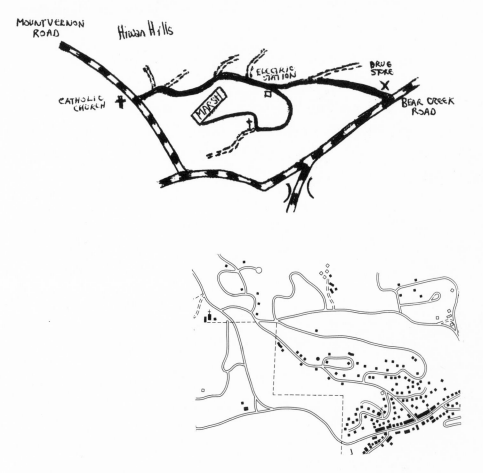

A homemade map (above) and an accurate map (below) of the same area.

but it is surrounded by many other houses which look equally important. Each house is the correct distance and direction from every other house. The roads run in the proper directions from each other.

Visitors to Washington, D.C., would want a map locating the White House, the Washington Monument,

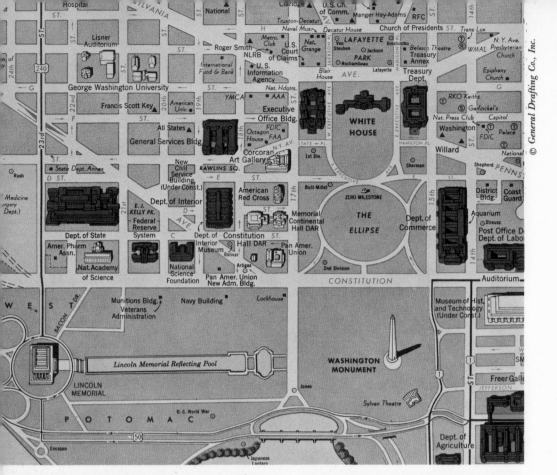

One inch on this map stands for 1135 feet on the ground. You could walk that far in less than five minutes.

and the Lincoln Memorial. Compared to the mountain-cabin map, the map on this page takes about four times as much space to show the same amount of ground.

A family planning an all-day picnic couldn't use any of these maps. An automobile would drive right off the Washington map in five or six minutes—unless it met a parade. Yet, using the same amount of space on the paper, a typical road map could show enough land for several hours of driving.

For a jet pilot, none of these maps would do. He would be off one of these maps almost before the sound of his plane reached the ground. To plan his flight, he would use a map showing much more of the earth.

SQUEEZING THE LAND

So, in choosing a map, the first thing to notice is how

One inch on this map stands for 79 miles on the ground. This is part of a jet pilot's planning chart.

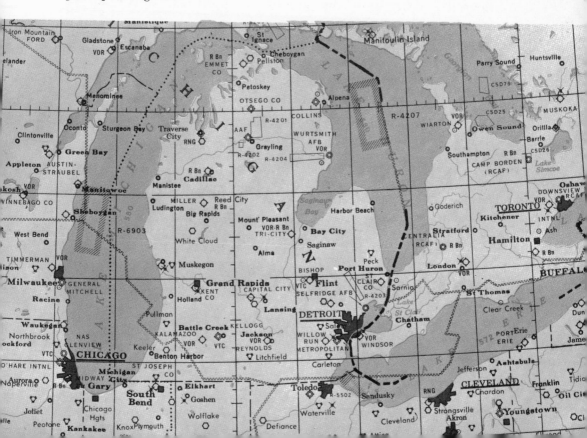

much the mapmaker left out. How much did he squeeze the land to make it fit onto his paper?

Imagine that the mapmaker has a globe like a balloon. Imagine that he can blow it up to be as big as the whole earth. Then the distance on the balloon globe will be the same as the distance on the earth. From San Francisco to Boise, Idaho, will be about 541 miles on either the earth or the balloon.

Now imagine that he lets so much air out of the balloon that the distance between San Francisco and Boise shrinks to about 541 inches. That means that one inch on the balloon will represent one mile on the earth.

Usually a map carries an explanation of how much smaller it is than the ground it pictures. A measuring stick, called a *scale,* is often printed on the map. You can measure a winding route by fitting a string along the route and then measuring the string on the scale.

There are two other ways mapmakers can explain how much the land is squeezed to fit the paper. One way is by saying how many inches represent a certain number of feet or miles. The mapmakers can say that the map is: "One inch to 1200 feet." Or, "One inch to ten miles."

Another way to show scale is to say on the map, for example, "1:112,000." This means that a person can take any unit, such as the length of his own thumb, as a measuring stick. If you measured a distance of two thumbs on the map you would know that the corresponding distance on the ground would measure twice 112,000, or 224,000 thumbs.

Maps like the jet pilot's show places that are far apart on the earth. They are called *small-scale* maps.

Using a *large-scale* map for a trip, you'll get lost unless you can imagine yourself as a tiny speck traveling across the map. A skilled map reader may turn a map upside down—or in any direction—to make it easier to read. To help decide where you fit on the map, you can often see some landmark that is shown on the map.

Mapping
the Earth

Who makes new maps? How do they know where to put each town? How do they know where the roads lead?

MAP EXPLORERS

Making a brand-new map is one kind of exploring. Someone must draw a picture of the way the ground actually is. One of the oldest sciences in the world is measuring distances on the ground—*surveying*. In Egypt the annual floods of the Nile River often washed away boundary marks. The rope-stretchers, as surveyors were then called, would relocate the boundaries in their proper positions.

The ways of exploring to make a basic map have changed a great deal, mostly within our own century. Today's mapmakers use planes, helicopters, trucks, and even mountain-climbing scooters. Yet there are still times when mapmakers need to be as rugged as the old-time explorers. They may crawl up big rocks on their hands and knees, with their equipment strapped to their backs.

The history of the world, from early times right up to this minute, is full of the adventures of the bold explorers who brought back maps of where they had

At times, mapmakers must still study the earth's surface the hard way.

been. Two early Presidents of the United States, George
Washington and Thomas Jefferson, were directly involved in mapping.

Washington earned money as a surveyor. His survey
office has been restored on a farm near Washington, D.C.

When Jefferson bought the Louisiana Territory from
France, nobody knew much about the land. Jefferson
sent his private secretary, Meriwether Lewis, and Captain William Clark of the U.S. Army to explore. They
brought back maps, studies of the Indian tribes, and
descriptions of the land. They also explored beyond the
boundaries of the Louisiana Purchase in the northwest.
That helped give the United States a claim to the
Oregon Territory forty years later.

THE TROUBLESOME COMPASS

In 1785, before the U.S. Constitution was adopted,
Jefferson helped the Continental Congress to set up a
special system for dividing public lands in the west.
There would be regular boundaries and square plots of
land.

When surveyors went to work, they found how hard
it is to divide large tracts of land into squares that will
fit together. As settlers moved west, the Bureau of Land
Management would establish two lines to guide the
local surveyors. One line ran east and west, the other

north and south. All the square plots of land were supposed to have their boundaries running those directions, too. Sometimes the surveyors made mistakes. But the legal boundary remains where it was first drawn.

Carelessness was seldom to blame. Sometimes the surveyor used an inaccurate instrument. More often his compass caused the trouble.

The compass is very useful—to someone who understands what it can and cannot do. In a few parts of the world a compass does point true north toward the North Pole, but in most places it does not.

The direction the compass points at any one place on earth keeps changing—not necessarily in a regular pattern. For about thirty years, in some parts of the world, the compass has pointed farther west each year. It has changed twice as fast in Europe as in the United States. In Canada and in the United States special government departments publish maps every five years showing what direction the compass points.

Early mapmakers and explorers could tell when their compasses did not point to the North Star—if the error was large enough. When Columbus sailed west, the error was so slight around the Mediterranean Sea that most seamen thought the compass always pointed north. Columbus knew better. But his crew almost mutinied as they noticed that the compass pointed farther away

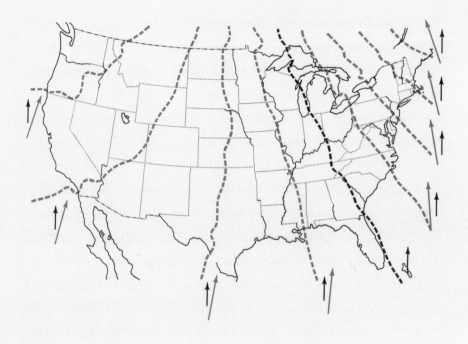

If you are anywhere on the black line, your compass will point directly north (black arrow). If you are on one of the blue lines, your compass will point in the direction shown by the blue arrow.

from the North Star each day.

There is also a daily change in the compass. Suppose a man draws a 1000-foot boundary line by compass at 8 A.M., marking each end of the line with a stake. Then his neighbor decides to check the line by compass at 1 P.M. His final stake is three feet away from the first man's stake. Which man is right?

Both of them—for the daily change in the compass

can make that much difference.

Besides the expected daily change, there are sudden magnetic "storms" related to sunspots. Then compasses everywhere become inaccurate by a degree or two.

Some kinds of underground rocks are magnetic and will deflect a compass.

MARKERS FOR MAPS

There is a more accurate way of making all the pieces of maps fit together. Markers can be set in the ground. The distance and direction from one to another can be carefully measured. Anyone in the United States can find a survey marker within a few miles of home.

In this part of the Rockies, a surveyor thought he was mapping mile-square sections. But underground magnetic rocks affected his compass.

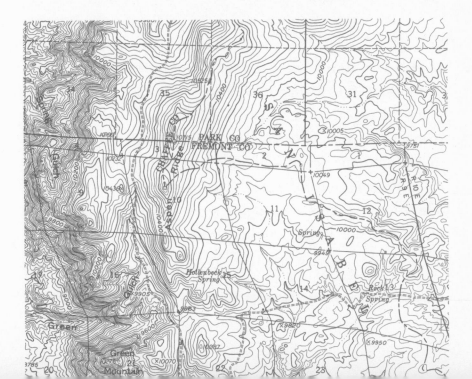

The round metal marker usually gives the name of the government organization which put it there. The Coast and Geodetic Survey—under the U.S. Department of Commerce—places the basic network of carefully measured markers. The Geological Survey—under the U.S. Department of the Interior—sets additional markers for mapping. Other organizations, such as the Bureau of Land Management, also set markers for boundary lines.

When men make roads, or locate boundary lines, or put up buildings, they start measuring from one of these markers. There are lists and diagrams of all the markers within a certain area, giving their distance and direction from each other. The basic network of markers is finished in the United States. But they are so far apart that thousands of additional markers are placed every year in the spaces between.

All of North America and part of South America are tied into a single network, with the key marker located at Meade's Ranch near Lucas, Kansas. On other continents there are similar networks.

The basis for the network of markers is the simple triangle. Anyone who studies enough math learns a way to find out the lengths of all three sides even if he can measure only one of them. He measures from A to C. Then he measures the angles at A and C. Then he can figure out the length of the other two sides.

Mapmakers call their measured line the *baseline*. The other two sides of the triangle may be across swamps or rough hills. Often tops of mountains are used, because then there can be a whole series of triangles to points close by and far away. Each new-found length of the side of a triangle can be used as the baseline of a new triangle.

The most accurate angle measurement can be done at night, using lights. In Alaska and in northern Canada, where summer nights are very short, it can be difficult to find enough dark hours.

Until recently, baselines were always measured on the ground. Early surveyors used a chain. Recent ones used a special nonshrinking steel tape. New methods measure the time it takes a light beam or a radio wave to travel from one place to another. The new devices can measure long distances, even over water. An instrument called the Geodimeter makes it possible to measure the camera locations for tracking missiles at Cape Canaveral with almost unbelievable accuracy.

Anyone measuring his own land would not need to

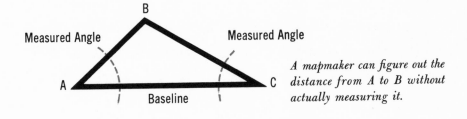

A mapmaker can figure out the distance from A to B without actually measuring it.

worry about the curvature of the earth. He could measure his property as if it were perfectly flat. For a small section of the earth *is* almost flat, and most surveyors measure that way. But a straight line from Boston to San Diego would have to plow through the earth. At Kansas City, Missouri, the line would be about 235 miles underground.

The checkerboard pattern of our western lands does not fit perfectly on the round earth. At regular intervals there are sections which are not square. Even so, there were a few places where different mapmakers came together—and their maps didn't fit. So wedge-shaped pieces were needed.

MEASURING HEIGHTS

The government's survey markers take into account the curvature of the earth, as well as the irregular high and low spots on the earth's crust. But to measure how high or low the spots are, there needs to be something from which to measure. So mapmakers use an imaginary sphere, called the *geoid*. This is the earth with all its bumps smoothed off—as if sea level continued under all the continents.

To get true distance between the survey markers, it is necessary to know how they compare in height above the imaginary geoid. All over our continent, a second network of markers—called *bench marks*—measure height. Very few actually give the height on the marker, because as instruments get more accurate it is sometimes necessary to correct the figure. The bench mark usually tells where to write for the latest information about its height.

There are various instruments, such as altimeters, which tell approximate height above the ocean. But the weather affects their accuracy. A specially equipped truck can measure the angle of a slope and the distance traveled at that angle.

But there still is no generally accepted, highly

Placing a bench mark.

accurate way of measuring heights except a very time-consuming one. This work is done by a group of specialists known as a *leveling party*.

One man sets up an instrument at the edge of the ocean. Farther inland another man holds a long stick upright. A certain place on the stick will be as high above the ocean as the eyepiece on the instrument. A man looking through the level telescope can read a number on the stick. If the eyepiece on the telescope is four feet above the ground, and the spot on the stick is three feet, the ground at the stick is one foot high.

Some heights have been measured by the triangle method. Because the atmosphere bends light, the angles should be measured in both directions. That is impossible on Mount Everest, for which careful surveyors get

The men of a leveling party usually work farther apart than this.

different results. The official height is 29,028 feet, as measured by the Indian Survey. That is closer to the height used a hundred years ago (29,002) than it is to the height still given in some encyclopedias.

Height above sea level is important, as we have seen, to people trying to escape a hurricane's high tides. Mountain climbers also like to know exact heights. In Colorado, a few years ago, some peaks were remeasured. People who had climbed all fifty-two of the peaks over 14,000 feet now needed to climb two more.

It saves money if the same marker can fit into both networks—the network of heights and the network of distance and direction. That seldom happens, except in flat country. The height network usually follows up valleys, while the distance-and-direction network uses mountaintops and hilltops. Both kinds of markers are set in concrete or solid rock.

Whenever a new road or building threatens to destroy a marker, someone should write to the government agency involved. It costs very little to place a new marker in a safer location while the old marker still exists. Later it may cost from $40 to $1500 to replace the destroyed marker. The government now spends over $125,000 a year replacing markers whose destruction no one bothered to report.

Guideposts
in the Sky

Suppose you find a survey marker placed by the U.S. Geological Survey or the U.S. Coast and Geodetic Survey. It will say: "For information write the director Washington, D.C."

If you write for information, what will you find out?

If your marker is part of the height network, you'll learn how many feet it is above sea level.

If the marker belongs to the distance-and-direction network, you'll receive two sets of numbers. One set is to help surveyors who measure fairly small areas within your state. The other set fixes the position of the marker on the earth. With those numbers alone, someone in India or Japan or Sweden could tell exactly where to locate your marker on a world map.

Here are the numbers for the most important marker in North America—the one at Meade's Ranch in central Kansas:

latitude   39°13'26".686 N
longitude 98°32'30".506 W

Later in this chapter, we will see what these numbers mean.

Over the centuries, men have devised a system for locating places on the earth. They learned to do it by studying the sun, moon, planets, and stars. Men gradually learned the answers to these questions: What shape is the earth? How big is it? How do you describe the location of a spot on the earth?

EARTH'S SHAPE AND SIZE

The most important discoveries were made long ago, in men's minds. Before the time of Christ, men had formed a better idea of the size and shape of the earth than anyone had again until after Columbus. For in the Dark Ages barbarians swept over the intelligent people living near the Mediterranean Sea. Magic and superstition replaced thinking.

At least three observations proved to the early thinkers that the earth is round. First, the top of a faraway ship or tower comes into view first. Second, in the northern hemisphere, stars that set below the horizon at one spot remain always above the horizon if you travel north. Third, when the earth gets between the sun and the moon, the earth casts a curved shadow on the moon.

Some men, then, long ago realized that the earth is round. They knew that it must be much larger than the areas familiar to them. It was a great achievement to measure the size of the earth before it had been explored.

This achievement was accomplished about 240 A.D. by Eratosthenes, head of the library in Alexandria, Egypt. Like a modern mapmaker, he used angles to find a distance without actually measuring it on the ground.

Eratosthenes discovered that at noon on June 21, the sun was directly overhead at a town called Syene. There the sun cast no shadow. But straight north, at Alexandria, the sun at that same moment was not directly overhead. It did cast a shadow.

By measuring the angle of the shadow, Eratosthenes decided that the distance from Syene to Alexandria was $\frac{1}{50}$ of the distance around the earth.

He figured that the earth must be 250,000 stadia around. We think that about ten of his stadia equal one of our miles. So his distance around the earth would be 25,000 miles.

This result was almost perfect—better, in fact, than his instruments justified. His inaccuracies balanced each other. Later, other men discovered some of these inaccuracies. When they tried to correct them, the results were less accurate. Columbus used the latest figures for his time, which made him think that the earth was only 18,000 miles around. That is why he thought he had reached the East Indies when he had sailed only as far as America.

HOW FAR NORTH OR SOUTH?

How would you describe the location of a spot on a round ball? First you would have to divide the ball into imaginary sections.

Should the sections be like thin slices of a tomato, or wedge-shaped sections of an orange?

Mapmakers use both methods. First they cut imaginary "tomato slices" through the earth. These result in lines of *latitude,* called *parallels.*

Where do you start measuring latitude? The North and South Poles are the points around which the earth rotates once a day. Halfway between the Poles an imaginary line—the Equator—circles the earth. This is the longest parallel of latitude. It is called "zero latitude."

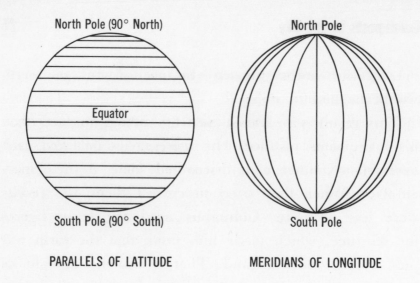

North Pole (90° North)

Equator

South Pole (90° South)

PARALLELS OF LATITUDE

North Pole

South Pole

MERIDIANS OF LONGITUDE

Half of the parallels are measured north from the Equator to the North Pole. Any circle can be divided into 360 equal parts called *degrees*. The North Pole is 90 degrees north—often written as 90° North.

The other parallels are measured south from the Equator to the South Pole, which is 90° South.

The parallel numbered 42 North forms the southern boundaries of Oregon, Idaho, and most of New York.

Each degree of latitude can be divided into 60 smaller units, called *minutes*. Each minute can be further divided into 60 units called *seconds*. With the use of decimals, the latitude of a spot on the earth can be given very precisely. The latitude of the marker at Meade's Ranch, given at the beginning of this chapter, means: "39 degrees, 13 minutes, 26.686 seconds north of the Equator."

Latitude has always been easy to find. In the northern hemisphere, the North Star is one guide. The farther north you go, the higher this star appears in the sky. The sun at noon is another guide. For two thousand years, men have been measuring the height of the North Star or the noonday sun. Today's instruments and tables are more accurate than ever before.

HOW FAR EAST OR WEST?

Mapmakers also divide the world into imaginary wedges like the sections of an orange. The resulting lines, which run from the North Pole to the South Pole, are lines of *longitude*. These lines are called *meridians*.

Meridian means midday—the moment when the sun reaches its highest point in the sky. Places on the same meridian of longitude have midday at the same instant. When it is midday in Memphis, it is midday in New Orleans. About an hour earlier, it was midday in Ottawa and Philadelphia.

How can mapmakers measure the difference in longitude between one place and another? For a very long time this could not be done, because time in one place could not be compared with time in another place.

Long ago people told time by sundials. If a traveler or mapmaker took his sundial to a place on another meridian, the sundial kept sun time for the new location.

Even the invention of the clock in the 1300's did not help much. An early clock had an hour hand, but no minute hand. A mapmaker could take a clock to a new location. But when he compared it with sun time in the new location he couldn't measure the difference more accurately than within an hour.

Centuries later, after clocks acquired minute hands, finding longitude was still partly guesswork. Clocks were not very accurate. If noon by the height of the sun occurs only one minute apart in two different places, they may be on different meridians sixteen miles apart.

Modern scientific mapmaking really began under King Louis XIV of France. He hired scientists from many countries, including an Italian named Giovanni Domenico Cassini.

For his mapmaking, Cassini used objects in the sky, hundreds of millions of miles away from the earth. These were the planet Jupiter and its moons, which Galileo had discovered after developing the telescope. From the earth, we see the moons eclipsed when Jupiter gets between them and the sun. At least two of the moons are eclipsed every two days. If observers at different places on earth watch one of these eclipses, they will see it happen at the same time.

Cassini had published tables telling when the eclipses of Jupiter's moons would occur. He gave the time in sun time where he was. Anyone who found an eclipse taking place at the same sun time as in Cassini's table would know that he was on the same meridian as Cassini. Other scientists could figure out how far east or west of Cassini they were. For they knew that 4 minutes of difference in sun time would place them one degree of longitude east or west of Cassini's meridian.

Observers all over the world sent Cassini their results. In 1679 he constructed a tremendous map at the Paris Observatory. Now, for the first time, maps became as accurate in longitude as they had been in latitude.

There was still one problem about longitude. From the time of Cassini, mapmakers agreed which meridian ran through a certain place. But for two centuries they refused to agree on a system for numbering the meridians.

The meridians, running from North Pole to South Pole, are all the same length. Nothing singles out one meridian as more important than another. So a Frenchman used to measure longitude east or west of the Paris Observatory. A Spaniard measured from Madrid. In the United States, old maps show Philadelphia as on the zero meridian. Later, when Washington became the capital, Washington was on the zero meridian.

Finally, in 1884, twenty-five nations agreed to start numbering east and west from Greenwich, England.

Today it is easier than ever to find longitude with

great accuracy. That is why the longitude of the marker at Meade's Ranch can be given with such precision— 98 degrees, 32 minutes, 30.506 seconds west of Greenwich.

By means of radio, scientists in England and in the United States can now coordinate their time within a thousandth of a second.

MAPPING BY SATELLITE

The basic network of latitude and longitude was settled long ago. But the job of fitting individual places into the network is far from finished. Today satellites are helping to determine the latitude and longitude of places on earth—especially islands.

It is easier to measure the angle to a satellite than to the sun or a star because the satellite is so much closer. As it orbits the earth several times a day, it can furnish many measurements for additional accuracy. And a satellite broadcasts its signals night and day in any weather.

Satellites have also supplied new information about the exact shape of the earth. As a satellite circles the earth, its orbit varies because of the stronger pull of gravity where the earth is bulkier. Mapmakers knew that the earth was slightly flattened at the poles. But until they studied the orbits of Explorer I and Vanguard I, they did not agree on how much it was flat-

For many centuries, people have found their position on earth by measuring the angles to stars. Today it is even easier to measure the angles to artificial satellites.

tened. Then the distance around the earth at the Equator was shown to be 12½ miles greater than the distance around the earth at the poles.

Some small irregularities came as a surprise. The North Pole bulges up about fifty feet, while the South Pole sinks in fifty feet. In the northern hemisphere the

earth is about fifty feet narrower than had been expected, and in the southern hemisphere fifty feet wider.
So the earth as a whole is slightly pear-shaped.

The Transit satellites have also proved that the
Equator is not a perfect circle. The Equator bulges out
about 500 feet in the eastern Atlantic and another 500
feet in the mid-Pacific.

Planning
a New Map

Since the early days of mapmaking, photography and the airplane have changed mapmaking completely. Mapmakers of today send up planes to take pictures of the ground.

In a few hours a plane with a camera can photograph as much land as a group of men used to map in months of working on the ground.

Today all new maps start as photographs.

At first glance, a photograph may look like a good substitute for a map. Someone who lives in San Francisco could recognize Nob Hill and Fisherman's Wharf from the photograph below. Perhaps by consulting the map in his head he could identify Chinatown. Others couldn't.

The map of the same area helps anybody find those places.

A map includes information missing from a photograph—names, directions, and distances. A map is clearer than a photograph. It emphasizes what is important.

The San Francisco map is a simplified map of a special kind—a topographic quadrangle map.

Photograph of downtown San Francisco.

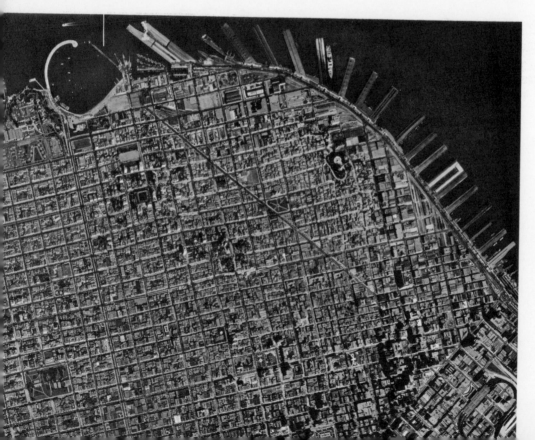

The term *quadrangle* refers to any shape of four corners and four sides. In quadrangle maps, the straight sides are based on lines of latitude and longitude.

The term *topographic* comes from the Greek *topos*, "place," and *graphikos,* "written." A topographic map shows the shape of the land in all directions—up and down as well as sideways. (The topographic detail, which will be discussed later, has been omitted from the San Francisco map here.) A topographic quadrangle map is often called a *quad map* for short.

Anyone planning to build a road, locate a factory,

Map of downtown San Francisco.

prepare for a hurricane—or make another map—starts by trying to find quad maps. It could cost thousands of extra dollars to find out what a quad map tells at once.

MAPPING THE UNITED STATES

In the United States, the Geological Survey is responsible for the quad maps.

The government mapmakers hope, by 1980, to complete detailed quad maps of every part of the country. These are on a scale of 1:24,000 (one inch to 2000 feet). Each will cover about 8½ miles from north to south. The distance from top to bottom of this page would represent less than three and a half miles. Sixty-four of

Well-mapped areas of the United States (except Hawaii) and Canada are shown in blue.

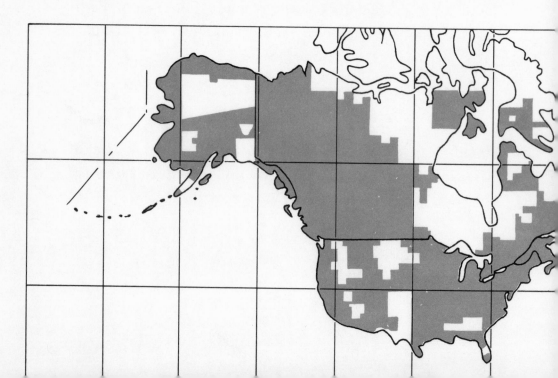

these maps will cover the area bounded by one degree of longitude and one degree of latitude.

The total project will require 32,000 of these very large-scale maps. About 22,000 are finished—but each year some of those need revising. By 1980 probably most of those now in use will have had to be replaced.

In any series of quad maps, all the maps will be the same size from top to bottom of the page, for latitude lines are just about the same distance apart everywhere on earth. But in the same series the widths of the maps will differ. A meridian comes closer to its neighboring lines as it approaches the Poles. Consider for example, meridians 80 and 81 West. Near Miami, Florida, there are 62 miles between the two longitude lines. Almost straight north, at Pittsburgh, the same two lines are only 53 miles apart.

One popular series of quad maps is at the smaller scale of 1:250,000 (one inch to about four miles). Each map covers one degree of latitude and two of longitude; 461 maps cover the United States.

STARTING A NEW MAP

Years ago a small group of men could make a U.S. quad map from start to finish. They spent months, drawing the map in the field as they traveled from place to place. The printed map had their names on it.

Some men did such accurate work that it is hard to improve on, even with much better equipment.

But maps need to be brought up to date. New roads appear. Towns grow. Dams turn a river into a lake. In deciding which old map needs to be remapped first, mapmakers study the changes and the demands in each area. But the deciding factor may be: Who made the old map?

Today a new map is the product of a large team. The U.S. Geological Survey divides the United States into four regions, with about 460 men and women working for each region, and about a hundred more in the Washington headquarters. Each region maps its own area. The mapping facilities are in Arlington, Virginia; Rolla, Missouri; Denver, Colorado; and Menlo Park, California.

To see the Geological Survey mapmakers in action, let's follow one quad map from start to finish. In this chapter and the next two, we will watch the preparation of the quad map for Rifle, Colorado.

In charge of the Denver office of the Geological Survey is the Regional Engineer of the Topographic Division. He is responsible for the successful completion of all the maps in his area.

Under him, in the Planning Section, about 15 highly trained engineers plan where and how the mapping will be done. At any one time about 100 men, led by field engineers, will be out in the field. They work in the southern part of their region in winter, and go north in summer. They hire other helpers locally.

In the Compilation Section, about 200 men and women produce accurate maps from air photographs.

Then in the Cartographic Section, about 80 more work on the final drawings.

A map usually takes two years from start to finish. To prepare a basic quad map, the mapmakers combine all the facts they can learn about the surface of that section of the earth, and where it fits into the whole earth. They combine mapping from the ground up with mapping from the air down.

PHOTOGRAPHS FOR MAPS

The Planning Section figures out what needs to be done, how to do it, and in what order. They study all the detailed maps that have ever been made of the area. They fit the new map into place with every other map around it, and with the framework of latitude and longitude.

The Planning Section often hires specialists in aerial photography. Usually several quad maps will be prepared at the same time. One airplane flight can cover an area large enough for several large-scale quads.

For the Rifle quad, the Planning Section orders the photography. They tell the pilot how high to fly, and how far apart to space his flights as he goes back and forth across the area.

The pilot uses a special camera. He sets its automatic shutter so that each picture will show more than half of the same land that is shown on any neighboring picture.

The pilot knows that if any of the photographs are not clear, he will have to do that part of the flight again. So he waits for a perfect day—no leaves on the trees, little or no snow on the ground, no clouds to make shadows, and no wind to bump the plane off course either up, down, or sideways.

The long roll of film in the automatic camera takes pictures nine inches square. So each picture is as long as this page and about two inches wider. Four of the pictures taken for the Rifle quad, plus two half pictures, could cover all the land in the whole quad. But because of the overlapping, the camera takes twenty-four photographs of the area.

GROUND CONTROL

The aerial photographs must be fitted into the network of markers that show latitude, longitude, and height. Those carefully located points—and others added by the field party—are known as *ground control*.

For study purposes, two sets of full-sized prints are made from the aerial camera's negatives. The actual mapping is usually done from smaller transparencies printed on glass. The reason is that glass can't stretch or shrink as paper can.

Each photograph print gets careful study. A planning engineer finds the center and pricks it with a needle. Then he finds at least three places in the photograph that a person with sharp eyes should be able to identify from the ground. He pricks each one, circles it with crayon, and labels it on the back of the photograph. An identification point might be where a fence meets a road, or a lone tree, or a rock on top of a hill.

Sometimes there are no landmarks, such as in a tremendous wheat field. Then the mapmakers may place a pile of stones or a target of cloth or plastic before photographing the area.

Since the pictures overlap, the same identification points will appear in several photographs.

On the next page is the planning work sheet for three quads. The Rifle quad is at the bottom right. This is a more complicated work sheet than most, for there are two sets of partly overlapping photographs, taken in different years. The center of each photograph is a circle with a number beside it. The survey markers belonging to the distance-direction network are triangles

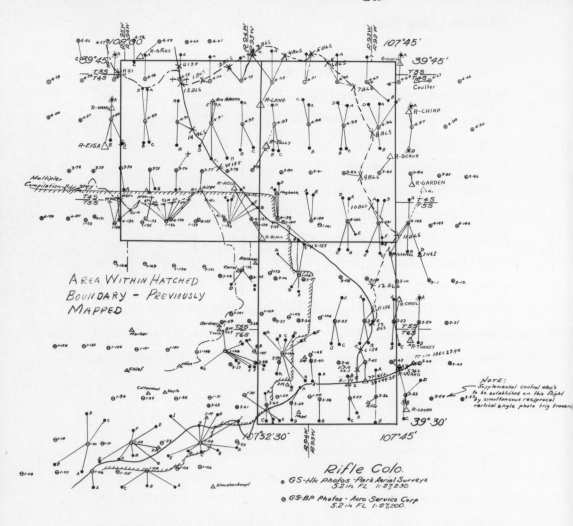

The planning work sheet for three quads, whose boundaries are straight lines. The Rifle quad is the rectangle at the lower right.

with names beside them. A dashed line across the top two quads and down the right side shows the route of the leveling party. Where they set bench marks are X's. The lettered dots are identification points.

On each quad, a small area has already been mapped, for it is part of a valuable Naval Oil Shale Reserve. That area, within the hatched boundary, needs only checking. Notice how the photography and the control points extend beyond the area to be mapped.

The field engineer and his crew of three or four men go to the area with all the photographs and the work sheet. By careful study, they locate on the ground all the identification points on the work sheet and on the photographs. The ground markers themselves are too small to show in a photograph. But they can be located if they stand at a conspicuous place, such as a spot where road meets fence. The field party measures from identification points to the most convenient survey markers. Later the latitude and longitude for the identification points can be figured out in the office, with the help of an electronic calculator.

The field party set additional markers as they measure, and make their own pricks and crayoned circles on the pictures where their new markers are. They try to find all types of boundary lines and locate them on the photographs. On the back of each picture they write any other information that could help the man who will transform the photographs into a map—the map compiler.

Compiling
a New Map

For mapping purposes, there probably has never been a perfect set of photographs. The same points on different pictures won't be the same distance apart. One picture may be tilted, or higher or lower than the others. Or a gust of wind may have swung the plane's tail so that the camera aimed in different directions. But, in the Compilation Section, there are ways to adjust the pictures to each other and fit things into their true position just as if the plane had flown an absolutely perfect course.

THE BASE SHEET

First there has to be an accurate *base sheet.* It covers the same area that the new quad map will cover. It must be more accurate than the field engineer's working map. A compiler draws the lines of latitude and longitude on a big sheet of paper-like plastic. Then, with extreme accuracy, he locates each point of known latitude and longitude—the survey markers. Many quads made from one set of pictures require many base sheets taped together.

On the base sheet two points are a known distance apart. The photographs have to be adjusted to fit. Paper photographs won't stretch or shrink at command, so an adjustable substitute has to be made for each one. It is called a *templet,* and is usually made of stiff plastic.

To make the templets a man uses a special machine. He transfers the marks on the photograph to the plastic templet. He cuts a hole in the corner. Then he cuts slots to represent each of the pricked identification points (including the corner holes of the adjacent pictures). Each slot points to the hole of its templet and extends on each side of the location of the picture point.

The templets overlap, just as the pictures do. Probably no two templets show two points exactly the same distance apart. The slots keep the identification points

24X

22X

courthouse clock

college cupola

police radio mast

79X

77X

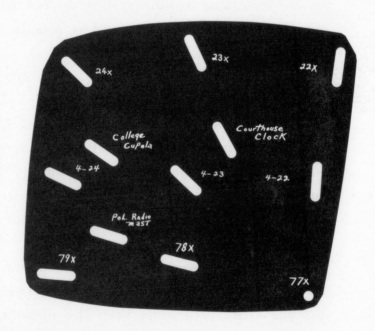

An aerial photograph (above) with its templet (below). By use of templets, overlapping photographs can be adjusted to exactly the same scale.

in the right direction from one another, but allow room for adjusting the distances between them.

Compilers set each templet in place on the base sheet. No table would be big enough to hold many base sheets taped together. So the men work on the floor. They take off their shoes to keep the base sheets clean while they walk around placing each templet.

Wherever there is a point of known latitude and longitude on the base sheet, the men cement a stud. Over that stud goes a slot in every templet that represents that same point. Some slots do not have a known position. But after five or six slots intersect there will

Placing templets on the base sheets for Big Delta, Alaska. The dark stripes represent lines of latitude and longitude.

be only one spot common to them all. At that point the men put another stud, and prick its location on the base sheet. Then that point, too, has a known latitude and longitude. As the men remove the templets they will circle and label each point on the base sheet.

In addition to templets, there is another method of adjusting photographs to each other and to the base sheet. This involves a long line of projectors. A projector can stretch a picture by showing it far away, or shrink it by moving closer.

The compiler adjusts the height and tilt of each projector as it shines down onto the base sheet. When each picture fits perfectly with its neighbors, and each ground point shines directly onto the spot on the base sheet where it belongs, the projectors will be reproducing the airplane's flight. Where the plane was too high, that picture's projector will be high. Where the plane was tilted, the picture's projector will be tilted.

When the pictures fit together, either from an assembly of templets or from an adjustment of projectors, it is time to turn the base sheet into an actual map. Now all the details between the known points of the ground control can be filled in from the photographs.

MAPPING WITH THE THIRD DIMENSION

A photograph gives a flat picture. It has only two dimensions—length and width. It has no depth. Each of your eyes also sees a two-dimensional picture. But because each of your eyes sees a little farther around an object, you are aware of its depth or thickness—its third dimension.

It would be difficult to get along without the third dimension. Try to shut one eye and toss an eraser in the air ahead of you. It will be hard to catch. With both eyes open there is no problem. The third dimension also helps us to understand true directions between things near and far away.

Modern mapmaking depends on three dimensions, in order to judge distances accurately and to put everything in its proper place. The three dimensions are achieved by means of stereo photography. Two slightly different pictures are used at once.

The two pictures are kept separate until they reach the compiler's brain, which fuses them into one three-dimensional picture.

The aerial photographs of Rifle were taken one at a time. But they overlap, so that parts of any two adjacent pictures can be used together to give a stereo effect.

Different mapping instruments use different ways to make each eye see only one picture at a time. Many systems use colored glass. Each of two projectors has a different colored filter, so that one picture will be pro-jected onto the base sheet in blue, while the other picture will be projected in red.

The compiler wears a special pair of glasses. One eyepiece is red; it makes the red picture invisible to that eye. The other eyepiece is blue; it makes the blue picture invisible to that eye. The compiler's brain combines the two separately viewed pictures into one picture which is black, white, and shades of gray. The picture is in three dimensions. The hills that appear to rise up above the paper look real enough to climb.

The compiler for the Rifle quad, using the latest methods, would start with a sheet of plastic with a yellow coating all over it. All the ground control would be on the map in its proper location. Instructions with the pictures tell him how to project them to make them fit in with the ground control.

First he draws all the roads. Or, to be more precise, he scrapes or *scribes* them. It is faster and more accurate to scrape the plastic's yellow coating off the sheet than it would be to draw something on it. It is something like scraping frost off a windowpane in winter. The compiler locates the true position of a road because he has a three-dimensional picture of it.

In scribing his lines, the compiler uses a *tracing table*. It looks like a small flat plate. Supporting the tracing table is a horseshoe-shaped base. A tracing

One photograph is projected in red, the overlapping photograph in blue (above). Wearing special glasses, the compiler sees on the plate of the tracing table (right) a three-dimensional picture of the ground. He moves the tracing table, keeping the central white dot on the part of the picture he is reproducing.

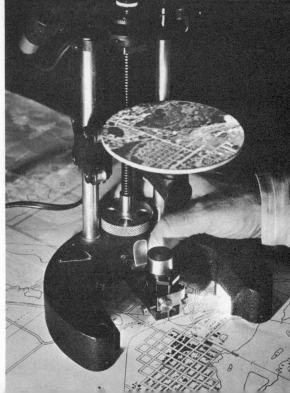

point below the plate scribes a line on the map as the operator pushes the tracing table, following a road on the three-dimensional picture he sees.

The compiler focuses the photographs on the plate of the tracing table. In the middle of the plate a "floating dot" appears. The dot is the important part of all three-dimensional mapping instruments. The operator can make adjustments so that the dot appears to rest on the ground shown in the center of the picture on the little tracing table. He can also make the dot appear to float through the air like a ball high above the ground, or even seem to be below the ground level. When the dot seems to be at ground level, the spot it touches will be in the proper position so that the tracing point can locate it on the base sheet just where it should be. Three dimensions put it in its place. So, in order to draw a road where it belongs, not too far right or left or front or back, the operator must keep adjusting the floating dot so that it skids along at ground level.

For Rifle, the compiler draws the roads. Then, in the same way, he traces both banks of the Colorado River, and the islands. As he keeps the floating dot at ground level, he locates the buildings in their proper places, too.

By now the map looks fairly complete, and many maps give very little more information. The San Francisco map on page 35 contains this much information. But the compiler makes two more plastic sheets for the Rifle quad. One shows where all the trees are. He draws a line around each orchard and traces the irregular outline of each patch of trees growing wild.

MAPPING CONTOUR LINES

The compiler's third sheet is the vital part of a quad map which makes it different from most other maps. It is the *topographic* part, which shows the shape of the land, the gentle slopes, the hills, and the mountains.

Most maps are frankly two-dimensional. A map-reader might guess that there must be a high point if all the rivers seem to run away from one part of the map. But is it a high mountain or a low hill? When two streams flow in the same direction not far apart, what keeps them from joining—a gentle slope or a steep ridge?

Through the ages, mapmakers have tried at least eighty different ways of showing hills. Some newspapers and some road maps still use a system invented by a famous Greek mapmaker, Ptolemy, about 150 A.D. He drew little pictures of hills which we now call "mole-hills." They show where the hills are, but not how high they are.

A better way of showing hills was developed in the seventeenth century. *Hachures* are little scratches which show which way the land slopes. When the lines are close together the hills are steeper than when the lines are far apart. But, like molehills, hachures cannot give an accurate idea of hill heights.

In 1791 a French mapmaker made the first land map showing exactly how high hills were. He used lines on his map to connect places that were an equal height above sea level. His *contour lines,* as they are now called, made mapping history. Canada and the United States and most other nations use contour lines on their quad maps.

Other maps may use contour lines of a sort. Different colors set off coastal lowlands from higher plateaus and still higher mountains. Where the color changes from dark green to light green, or from yellow to tan, there will be a line separating the two colors. This is actually a contour line.

At the edge of the ocean, high tide leaves an irregular line of seaweed and driftwood and shells, which is like a contour line. It shows where sea level was at high tide. If the tide should rise a foot higher than usual, the water would push the debris one foot higher on the beach. On a map, every contour line connects all points which would be at the water's edge if sea level rose by that many feet.

Quad maps are especially useful because of their information about the level of the ground. Very few

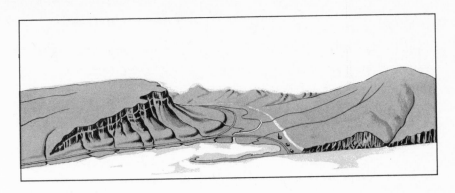

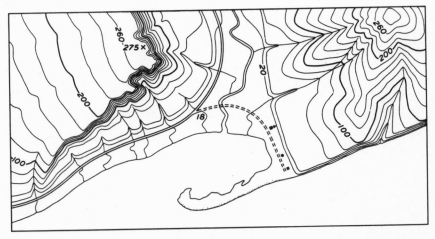

With practice, a map reader can picture the shape of the land (above) from looking at contour lines (below).

people need to know heights to escape a hurricane's high tides. But for many kinds of planning, from hikes to road building, it is important to know where the hills are—and how steep they are. A trained mapreader can picture the hills from looking at the contour lines.

All the early maps with contour lines were drawn by

field parties in the same way that bench marks are still placed—by measuring how much higher one spot is than another. In almost level country that is still the cheapest way. But for most maps, stereo photographs give better results in less time.

The floating dot is the key to drawing contour lines because the dot can find the level of the ground. When the compiler draws a road, he keeps adjusting the floating dot so that it stays at ground level as the road goes up and down hill. But he uses a different method to scribe the contour lines. He sets the dot at a certain height and leaves it there. Then he pushes the tracing table around the edge of a hill in such a way that the dot seems to stay always at ground level. During this operation, the point directly below the floating dot is scribing an irregular line on the base sheet. The tracing table connects everything at one height all the way around a hill, drawing a continuous contour line.

Then the compiler adjusts his floating dot so that it appears to touch ground forty feet higher—for that is the interval between contour lines on the Rifle quad.

On some quads the contour interval may be only five feet. On any quad map, there will be steeper ground where the contour lines are close together than where they are far apart. The Rifle quad has some very steep places.

Usually, to make it easier to check the compiler's work, all these sheets are printed on a single sheet of paper, but each in a different color—roads, trees, and contours. The compiler adds notes to his map asking the field party to check certain places. Perhaps the trees are so thick he can't put the floating dot at ground level. Or he may not be sure whether a certain line is a trail or a paved road. Other things in the pictures may need explaining. So, like every other Geological Survey quad map, the Rifle map gets a final check-up.

FIELD COMPLETION

A field engineer goes back to the Rifle area, taking the compiler's map. He finds out how names should be spelled to satisfy the people who live nearby. (On one Michigan map, that means spelling Mesabi in three different ways.) He classifies the roads—gravel, hard surface, or heavy duty. He classifies the buildings, so that schools will look different from churches, or houses, or barns. If a building has burned down since the aerial photography, he will cross it off the map.

All government boundaries must show on the quad map. The field engineer must find the boundaries, even the section lines dividing western land into one-mile squares. Some are found before compiling the map, some during the field check.

The field engineer checks the compiler's accuracy. A

certain proportion of the quad maps get an even more thorough examination to make sure the methods are producing accurate maps. Nine-tenths of the things shown on the map must be within $\frac{1}{50}$ of an inch of where they belong. That means within 40 feet of their location on the ground.

Sometimes a map flunks the test. Then someone has to correct the mistakes. At every stage there is constant checking to make sure that the map fits with other maps, with the photographs, and with the ground control.

Drawing
a New Map

When the Rifle map finally satisfies all the critics in the Denver regional office, it is ready to go to the artists and draftsmen of the Cartographic Section. They try to make every map not only accurate but also easy to read, as well as beautiful. The final map will be printed in many colors. Each color must have a separate printing plate. Like the map compilers, the draftsmen use scribing as they prepare the map for printing.

Many copies of the compiler's map are reproduced on sheets of coated plastic. Each draftsman works on one sheet. One makes the dark-blue printing plate. He

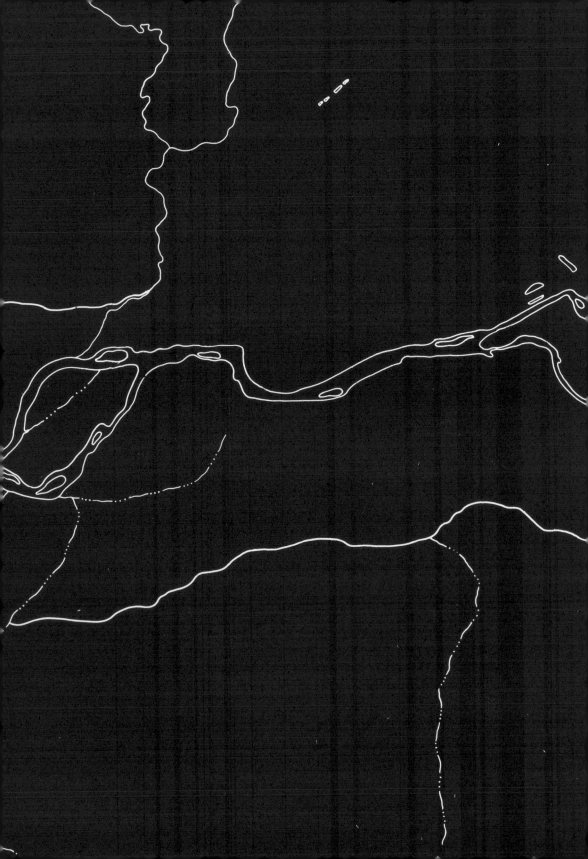

scribes all the water features. For small streams he scribes a single line. But for the wide Colorado River he scribes both banks and all the islands, large and small. He outlines the ponds and lakes. Streams that are usually dry in summer he shows by scribing a long line and then three dots, then repeating the pattern. Notice that one of those streams cuts across an island in the Colorado River, probably during high water in the spring. The Rifle quad gives the worker very little to do on the dark-blue plate. On other quad maps, marshes, swamps, or glaciers would go on this plate.

There is another blue plate for the Rifle quad—a light blue one to fill in large bodies of water such as the ponds and the Colorado River. It takes a lot of scraping with a different kind of tool—less like a needle, more like a little shovel.

This scribed plate shows streams, as well as the broad Colorado River with its islands. Every line shown in white on the negative will appear in dark blue on the final map.

The green plate takes the same kind of wholesale scraping. Like one of the compiler's maps, it will show all the groups of trees. While the compiler simply outlines the areas, the draftsman must show the difference between natural trees, growing as a forest, and others. For the forests he scrapes the area clean. For scrubby little trees he uses an irregular dotted pattern. For trees planted in rows, as in a fruit orchard, he scrapes the whole area clean, and then sticks onto the area a printed pattern of dots.

Many kinds of patterns are available on sticky paper. Sometimes it is easier to scrape off a wide hunk of coating and then press down a strip that contains a perfectly straight narrow line than it would be to scribe the narrow line, especially when the line is dashed or dotted. (There are special tools, however, for scribing interrupted lines.)

This plate shows forests (bottom) and orchards (top).

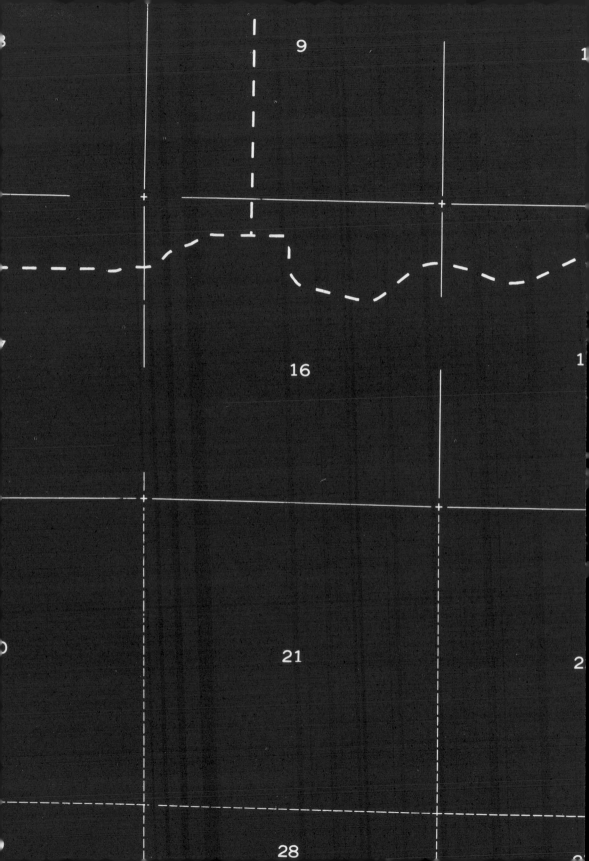

The red plate for Rifle could have been done either way. The thin red lines which make squares one mile on each side are the boundaries of sections, the systematic divisions of public land. The small crosses where the lines intersect show that the field men actually found the original mark for that corner. Where the section lines are dotted instead of continuous there is some doubt about the location of the line.

The wider lines are roads. Only good roads show on the red plate. Since on Rifle's quad there are no heavy-duty roads, the two best roads show as dashed lines. In a large city the built-up area would have a pattern of closely spaced red dots. But in the Rifle quad there is no big city.

This plate shows roads, section lines, and section numbers.

Every building appears on the black plate. Most of the symbols are easy to understand. Churches have crosses. Schools have flags. Houses will be solid black on the map.

The black plate is the first one that looks like a map, even before it is combined with the other plates on the printed map of many colors. The black plate shows principally what man has done. Roads, built by man, show on the black plate—even those which are also on the red plate, for they have double black lines to outline them. The railroads have bars across the black line to make them look different from roads.

Man provided names, so all the names are in black. In a few remote mountainous areas the only proof of man's presence is that the height of a mountain appears on the black plate—because someone was there to measure it. Every point on the Rifle quad is more than a mile above sea level.

On all the plates shortcuts are used. Numbers and names are printed on adhesive paper and stuck onto the map.

This plate shows man-made features, including buildings and names.

The brown plate looks very much like the compiler's contour-line drawing. It will be complete, instead of having places where the contour lines disappear into the trees. The draftsmen make every fifth line heavier, so it is easier to follow the same level around a hill. Every 200-foot contour has its height printed on the map in brown. Here the draftsman sticks numbers into place on the proper line.

The brown plate transforms the quad map into a "three-dimensional" map. Near the bottom of the map the contour lines bunch together in a steep cliff—which shows why the town of Rifle was built on the other side of the Colorado River. But the brown plate shows where man made some hills and valleys himself. The straight contour lines which follow the road in the upper right half of the brown plate have little short lines sticking out. Those mean a depression instead of a hill, and show where dirt was taken out to raise the road bed above the surrounding low land. Near the center of the brown plate there are short straight lines radiating from a central point. They show a high place where men dumped tailings from a vanadium mill. Some day the man-made land forms will look like natural shapes.

Road builders need to know where they can find gravel. The quad maps show it. Can you find the gravel beds along the Colorado River? The draftsman cleared the area and then stuck on a pattern of dots.

This plate shows the contour lines which give a quad map "three dimensions."

These examples show just a small corner of the whole Rifle map. Larger sections of the Rifle quad are illustrated on the end papers of this book.

Because all U.S. topographic quadrangle maps are printed in Washington, the plates for the Rifle quad are sent there. Finally all the finished, many-colored Rifle quad maps go back to Denver.

All maps west of the Mississippi River are stored in Denver until sold or replaced. Maps of the eastern United States are stocked and sold in Washington. About 5,000,000 maps are sold each year. The Geological Survey prints about 2,000 different maps in a year, two-thirds of them new or revised maps.

Some National Park maps, a few quadrangle maps, and a few state maps come in a special edition called *shaded relief*. It shows the shadows which would fall on the sides of the hills if a bright light were shining from the northwest. The shading makes the contour lines easier for an unskilled map reader to understand.

Road Maps

Even people who think they don't use a quad map really do—secondhand. Almost all maps of larger sections of the United States start with sets of government quad maps.

Road maps are a good example. Practically everyone looks at a road map occasionally. The gasoline stations each year give away as many road maps as there are people in the United States.

The road map begins from a lot of quad maps. A road map and a quad map are almost the same size. What they show is very different.

MAKING A ROAD MAP

To make a road map for New York State, one map company bought almost all the quad maps of the state. There are 925 separate maps listed on the Geological Survey's index of New York State quad maps. Some overlap. There may be four new maps covering the same area as one older map. Naturally, the mapping company will use only the newer, larger-scale maps.

Most of the details on a quad map have to be omitted from a road map, as the many quads shrink to fit into the road map. A photograph can reduce the size of the quad. A quad map would have to be reduced to one sixth its size to fit on a page of this book. Even that small size is too big for the road-map makers.

To make their work easier, the men make road maps twice as big while they are working on them, and let the camera reduce the drawing to final road map size. Even at twice the final size, the little negatives of quad maps are as hard to fit together as a jigsaw puzzle. A man eases the little pieces into place, building them into a map of the whole state.

The next step combines the patchwork of negatives onto one sheet of white paper. Every line from the quad maps shows, all printed in light blue. Of the jumble of lines, the draftsman decides which to trace over with black ink.

Nine quad maps have been photographed together and reduced to fit a page of this book. Ithaca, New York, is in the central quad.

To begin with, the road map will be only two-dimensional. That means omitting everything which belongs to the third dimension—the hills and valleys. All the contour lines are ignored. The wooded areas may look important on the negatives, but the mapmaker ignores them, too. He omits section boundaries, the names of crossroads such as Whipple Corner, and on most road maps the railroads. He will trace over the main roads, some of the side roads, the shape of the end of Lake Cayuga, the size of the town of Ithaca, the location of the airport, and the location of the two state parks.

On the quad maps, the scale is so large that every house can be shown. On the road map, the scale is so small that only a town of at least ten thousand people is large enough to be drawn to scale. Other towns show as dots—which take up more room on the map than the towns do on the earth. Different road-map makers use different systems for showing the size of the town by the kind of dot. All mapmakers use bigger type for towns with more people.

On the reduced quad maps, the roads become such thin lines that the mapmaker has to broaden them. (According to the scale of the road map, each road is drawn as if it were a half-mile wide.) The roads look straighter on the road map than they did on the quad maps, for the mapmaker does not trace every little twist

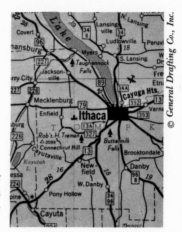

On the final road map, the nine quad maps cover only this much space. One quad map takes up less room than a postage stamp.

or turn. He calls this *generalizing* the lines.

Road maps are usually revised each year. There are always changes since the publication of the quad map. One man checks with the state's highway department to find out about new roads, new bridges, and new paving. Other men drive around the state as they believe typical tourists will do. They make sure that their map will be helpful on the most important routes. An annual revision of a map often includes about a thousand changes.

About every five years there has to be a completely new map, made again from basic quad maps. It costs as much to transform quad maps into a road map as it would cost to buy 80,000 quad maps.

When a town grows enough so that its name can appear in bigger type, the inhabitants expect the map

to show it. One man in the mapping company keeps
track of the latest census figures to make sure that the
maps are up-to-date.

When all the up-to-date facts have been collected, a
draftsman puts the finishing details on the map made
from the quad maps. When he draws a circle for a
town, he knows what to put inside the circle to show
how big the town is. He uses a special pen to draw
the circles. And he chooses a different style of type for
each category of names on the map.

USING A ROAD MAP

Even though many small towns shown on the quad
maps had to disappear from the final road map, more
than 2,500 remained on the New York State road map.
There is a list of all those towns, in alphabetical order.
After each town is a letter and a number showing
where to locate it on the map.

Numbers are important on a road map. Boxed numbers give route numbers. An Interstate Highway, on the
Arizona map, has a number set in a dark shield. A
Federal Highway has a number enclosed with an outline of a shield. The state highways have numbers set
in squares.

Other numbers give the mileage from one place to
another. Mapmakers put a scale on road maps. On the
Arizona map, an inch represents about fifty-seven

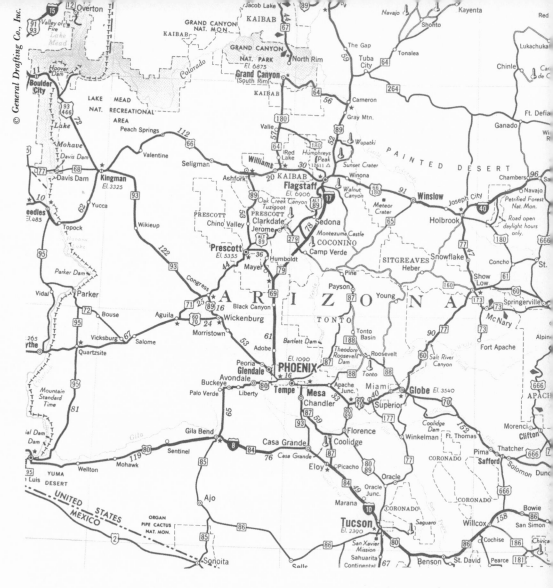

Road-map makers choose different type styles for different categories of names—for instance, Arizona, Flagstaff, Painted Desert, and Grand Canyon National Park.

miles. But the mapmakers use another system to make it even easier for a traveler to estimate distances. The mapmaker puts the distance between towns as he did between Tucson and Eloy, with a star at each end to show where he started and stopped measuring. Some of the distances are actual readings from a car speedometer, but many are figured from quad maps.

Of all the millions of road maps distributed by oil companies in the United States, nine-tenths are made by three companies: General Drafting Company (which made several maps used in this book); H. M. Goushá Company; and Rand, McNally and Company (which makes many other kinds of maps and sponsors international conferences on mapping). The American Automobile Association also makes some of the maps that it distributes.

The three road-map companies all make good maps. They keep working to make their maps more pleasant to look at, easier to read, and more crammed with interesting facts. The companies all claim that nothing else in print contains so many facts per square inch as a good road map.

The oil companies want each map to be so enticing that a motorist will start right out on a trip—for which he will need to buy gasoline. Each mapping company prints its own name, as well as the name of the oil company, on its maps.

The maps made by the three big companies differ in many respects. What the mapmaker chooses to keep from the quad maps is partly up to his own judgment. For one trip, a traveler may wish to have a map made by each of the companies. One may show more side roads. Another may have large-scale maps of big cities, or show where the new Interstate Highway System is finished, or give the lines of latitude and longitude. You can learn to tell one company's maps at a glance, just as you learn to tell the new models of different automobiles.

A filling-station attendant can tell you where to write for maps of other states, or how to get marked maps showing the best route for a trip. Some companies publish road maps of countries on other continents, too.

A road map is usually the property of the company which made it. Anyone who copied the map without permission could be forced to pay heavy damages. A map which must not be copied will say some or all of these things: "Copyright. All rights reserved. This work must not be copied in whole or in part."

Some road-map companies used to put "planted errors" on their maps, which were traps to catch anyone who copied the map. One company invented a town named Algoe, and planted it where the President and Vice-President liked to go fishing. Now mapmakers don't bother with planted errors. It would be easy to copy a road map by photographing it, but the copy would reveal its source in every line.

When you pick up a free road map, it probably costs the oil company between six and seven cents. This means that the oil companies give away millions of dollars worth of maps every year.

From Round Earth
to Flat Map

So far, most of the maps in this book have been large-scale maps. There has been no need to mention a major problem of mapmaking—the problem of *projection*.

A projection is a way of transferring the lines of latitude and longitude from the round earth to flat paper. It is an attempt to flatten out the surface of the tomato-like slices of latitude and the orange-like wedges of longitude.

A mapmaker will draw in lines of latitude and longitude even though he may erase them later. They help him to locate places in the proper section of the map. Should he draw these lines straight or curved? There's no perfect answer. There can't be. For latitude and longitude lines exist in three dimensions, while a flat paper map has only two dimensions.

GLOBES AND MAPS

All the meridians of longitude are circles of the same size. Each circle has two different numbers, for we think of a meridian as ending at each Pole. But the zero meridian which goes through Greenwich and the 180° meridian which is the International Date Line are simply two halves of the same circle around the earth.

The parallels of latitude are circles of different sizes. The Equator is about the same size as each meridian. Then, as you go north or south toward the Poles each parallel gets smaller (as shown on page 26).

A completely accurate world map should show all meridians the same length, and parallels of different lengths. Each of the lines should be in three dimensions so it could meet itself in a circle. The only map that can do all this is a globe.

Even a globe can be truly accurate only when it is hand-painted. Otherwise it, too, faces the problem of fitting something flat onto something round. Many globes have flat paper maps pasted onto a round ball. A close look will reveal places where the pieces don't fit perfectly. Usually there are twelve pieces called gores, with two circles to cover the polar areas.

There is a line of satellite-tracking stations placed along the 75th meridian west. When the globe faces you so that the 75th meridian looks straight, it is easy to see that a straight line south from the North Pole passes east of Hudson's Bay, between Montreal and Ottawa, through Philadelphia, through Columbia and Peru, and then into the Pacific Ocean until it reaches the islands west of southern Chile.

As you turn the globe, the same parallel changes from a straight line to a curved one. If you turned the globe so you could just see the 75th parallel at the far left or far right, it would look like a half circle.

Globes are awkward to carry around, and they are always far too small to show much detail. Flat maps have several advantages over globes. They can show more than half the earth at a time. They can show great detail. And they can be reproduced very cheaply.

But any map reader should always compare his flat map with a globe—even if it is just an imaginary globe.

DIFFERENT PROJECTIONS FOR DIFFERENT PURPOSES

If the area covered by a map is a small part of the globe, the mapmaker can make a flat map that looks accurate. The projection—the way he draws the parallels and meridians—makes very little difference.

Here are two projections of the continental United States—both frequently used. The Albers Equal Area Projection (shown in black) is useful for comparing the relative sizes of areas. The Lambert Conformal Conic Projection (shown in blue) is particularly useful to pilots because direction, distance, and area are all shown quite accurately.

Even the entire United States is a relatively small part of the whole earth. So there is no tremendous difference between various types of projection. The long section of the U.S.-Canadian boundary following the 49th parallel can be shown as a straight line, as in the map on page 36. Usually that parallel is shown as curved on U.S. maps—but the amount of the curve differs on different projections. You can see this on the two preceding pages.

Each of these frequently used projections is accurate. Yet when they are shown on the same page the difference is apparent. Each large, window-sized map is on the same scale—one to five million. The maps are placed to make them coincide in southern Texas and at Cape Flattery, the northwestern point of Washington State. The distance from San Diego, on the Pacific, to Boston on the Atlantic is 32¾ inches on one map, but 33 inches on the other. The maps are greatly reduced to fit on the pages of this book.

All projections have the same aim—to make a useful map. The mapmaker wants to show accurately the distances between places, or the direction they are from each other, or the size of one area in relation to another, or the true shape of each area. These can't all be shown at once. So each mapmaker chooses a projection that will be most useful for a particular map. At least two hundred different projections have been in-

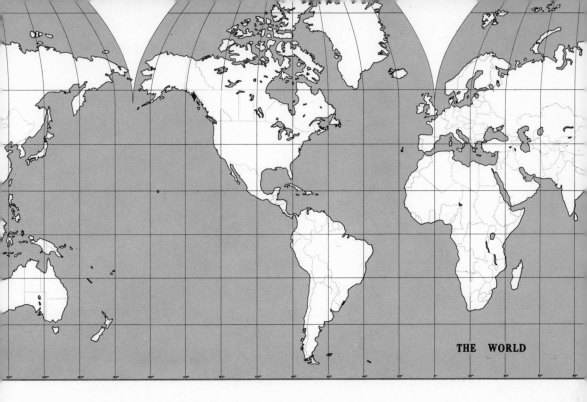

THE WORLD

A modified Mercator map, issued by the Canadian government.

vented. A persistent map reader can probably find a projection made to fit his special interest.

The most famous projection ever made was invented by Gerard Mercator in 1569. (It is used for the map on page 36.) Others had tried making all the parallels and meridians straight lines. Mercator's great invention was in spacing the parallels farther apart as they approached the Poles. That way he was stretching a globe equally in two directions.

Near the Poles, the Mercator projection becomes so

distorted that Greenland looks bigger than South America. There is no need to use a projection for a purpose which it doesn't fit, so a Mercator world map usually stops at the 70th parallels. Or it inserts some blank paper near the North Pole, and curves those meridians in the far north, while keeping the rest of the map in the Mercator projection.

In one respect, the Mercator projection is better than any other type of projection—and even more useful than a globe. A straight line drawn between any two places shows the exact compass direction between the two points. For that reason all navigators, especially on ships, use Mercator maps constantly.

Many projections are distorted at the edges, but more accurate nearer the center. But the center can be any place on the globe. Usually a Mercator projection is centered on the Equator. But it doesn't have to be. It could be centered on a belt that went diagonally around the earth, or on one of the meridians. Near the Poles, airplane pilots use a Transverse Mercator projection, centered on the meridians 0° and 180°.

A Mercator map is excellent for figuring directions. But it is useless for measuring distances, because each part of the map is at a different scale. Another projection is perfect for measuring the shortest distance and the true direction—but from just one place, the center of the map. The U.S. government publishes world maps

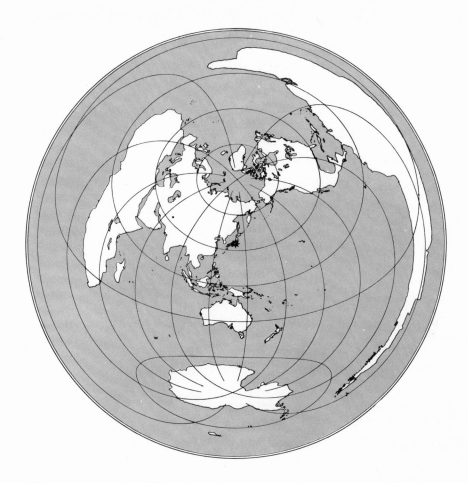

This map, centered on Tokyo, is perfect for measuring distance and direction— from that city only.

with various cities at the center—Tokyo, London, Seattle, New York, and other places.

Another projection shows the shortest route from one place to another. It is extremely useful in this air age. On a globe you can find the shortest route by stretch-

ing a string between the two points. You get a Great
Circle route. Any Great Circle, if continued around the
globe, would divide the globe into two equal parts.
The Great Circle projection shows that the shortest
route from the Panama Canal to Tokyo goes through
Texas, Oregon, and the Aleutian Islands in southwest
Alaska. A flier could use this type of map to plan his
route. Then he could transfer his route to a Mercator
map by finding the intersections of latitude and longitude every hundred miles. The Mercator map would
show him what compass direction to use every hundred miles. For there is still no instrument that can
guide the flier on a perfect Great Circle route.

A compromise map of the northern hemisphere is
much better for showing true shapes and true directions.
It is often used for maps centered on the North Pole.
One edge of the paper covers India, and the opposite
edge Mexico. South is at all sides. This projection
shows the Northern Hemisphere so well that it is be-
coming a very popular type of map, for nine-tenths of
all the people on earth live in the Northern Hemisphere.

Another projection is the principal one used by airplane pilots. It is true to scale along certain parallels.
The blue outline map of the United States on pages
84–85 uses this projection. It uses the parallel dividing
Kansas from Oklahoma as the most accurate part of the

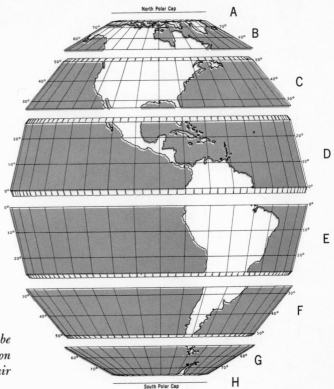

This is how a globe may be made, using the same projection that is used for almost all air charts.

map. On this type of map the straight-line distance is never more than 9½ miles away from the Great Circle route, although it is 170 miles longer between San Francisco and New York. (On a Mercator chart the true-direction distance would be 181 miles longer than a Great Circle route.) There is some distortion in this projection, but not much.

STRETCHING A MAP

Changing from one projection to another usually means

that the mapmaker must draw a new framework, and then fit places into the proper intersections of latitude and longitude. Air Force mapmakers experimented with another method for stretching a map into another projection. They printed the map on a sheet of rubber. Then they pulled the map so that it almost fitted the lines of another projection.

Every map reader should keep this process in mind. For any flat map stretches the globe in one way or another.

Charts
for the Sea

Only a landlubber refers to a map. A sailor or an airplane pilot always calls his map a *chart*. Nautical
charts are for travel by sea. They show the land at the
edge of the ocean; the land under the water, and how
deep the water is; the markers on and near the water
which help ships find their way.

In the early history of the United States, nautical
charts were as important as land maps. Most of the
trade between the thirteen colonies had been by sea,
but there were many shipwrecks. Safer shipping lanes
would lead to more trade among the states, and thus

tie them into a closer union. So President Jefferson founded the Coast Survey in 1807 to make accurate nautical charts. He recognized the importance of having the charts of water areas firmly tied into a network of survey markers on shore. Thus began the networks which now tie the continent into one framework.

Modern nautical charts show Gedney Channel as one of the main routes into New York harbor. If it had been known in 1778 the French fleet could probably have surprised and captured the British fleet, thus shortening the American Revolution.

CHARTING THE BOTTOM

While mapmaking and ships have changed greatly since the early charts were made, what the map reader wants is still the same—a safe route. The modern chart of the entrance to New York harbor shows the deep channels where large ships are safe. It also tells the depths all over the chart—just as the topographic quad map tells heights. Both use numbers and contour lines. In a nautical chart the contour lines are sometimes continuous lines. On the New York chart, instead, each line has an arrangement of dots. The three-dot line is in deeper water than the two-dot line.

Anyone can find out how deep water is. Tie a weight to one end of a rope, so that it will sink to the bottom. Pull up the wet rope and measure it. For

Section of the chart showing the approach to New York harbor.

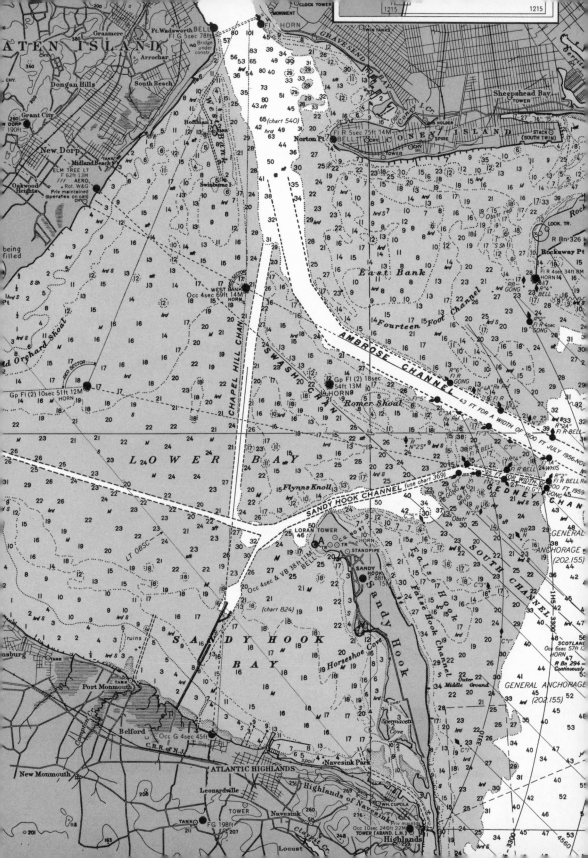

centuries that was the only way to measure depths, and
a slow process it was.

The quick way used today measures the length of
time it takes a sound to hit bottom and bounce back
up. Sound travels more than four times as fast in water
as in air, and makes a round trip of a mile in less
than two seconds.

An automatic depth recorder times the echoes. It

*Seagoing chartmakers of the Coast and Geodetic Survey study their automatic
depth recorder.*

makes a graph on a long roll of paper. At the end of a day the graph will be 75 feet long.

Because charts show the depth at low tide, the boat crew keeps track of the time. Later, when the chart is made, someone can figure out how high the water was above low tide when the echoes were recorded. Then the proper amount can be subtracted from each *sounding*, as a depth record is called.

Sounding finds all the depths along the line that the ship travels, but there is still room for a dangerous rock to lurk between lines of soundings. Near shore the sounding lines may be as close together as the width of a football field, but farther at sea the lines are farther apart.

Many places along our coasts have dangerous hazards. In Long Island Sound are many huge boulders washed down by glaciers in the Ice Age. Around Florida' are high, ragged masses of coral. Near New England and Alaska are great underwater mountains coming perilously near the surface. A submarine traveling up the west coast toward Alaska could find its way among the underwater mountains with the help of a special chart.

Where the bottom is dangerously irregular, two ships drag a long wire between them. It will stay at the proper depth after the weights and buoys attached to the wire are adjusted. The ships may work as much as

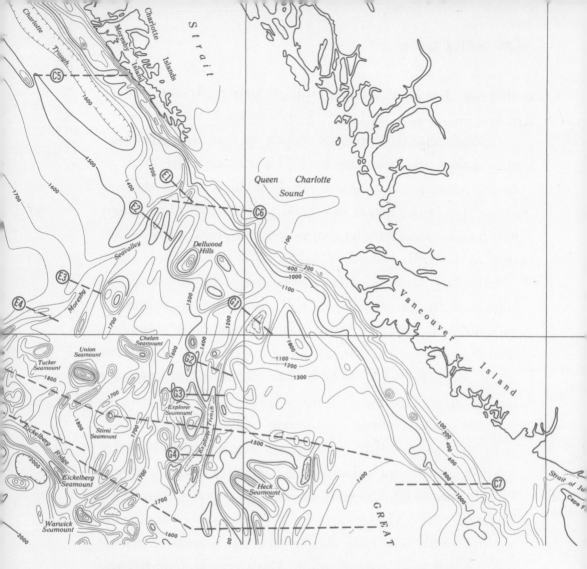

Chart showing undersea mountains and trenches off the coast of British Columbia. Dashed lines show routes for which profile diagrams are available.

three miles apart.

A ship with its own sounding device can keep track of the depth of the water and stay on the right course in fog or darkness. On any one chart all the depths will be given in the same unit. On some charts that will be in feet, on others it will be in fathoms. A fathom equals six feet.

A fleet of Coast and Geodetic Survey ships, large and small, are constantly collecting information to keep nautical charts up to date. But ships on other business sometimes discover facts that should be on a chart. The captain sends the information to the Coast and Geodetic Survey. The first submarine to go under the North Pole discovered some new underwater mountains and valleys which now appear on charts.

Charts show the location of wrecks of old ships. Large vessels stay away. But wrecks attract another group of people. They put on a face mask and flippers, strap a tank of compressed air on their backs, and swim down to hunt for treasure. Nautical chartmakers sometimes use the same kind of equipment.

PHOTOGRAPHS FOR CHARTS

Like mapmakers on land, chartmakers of today find that photography is one of their most useful techniques. Black-and-white photographs used in pairs help make three-dimensional charts of the land at the water's edge. The photographs are tied in with ground survey markers, just as quad maps are. To find the exact shoreline at high or low tide, infra-red photographs are best.

Channels show best in color photographs, for deep water will be a different color. Color photography makes it possible to plot the underwater depths in clear Caribbean waters as much as seventy feet below the surface.

Color photographs save time in locating the 24,000 floating signals or buoys that must appear on charts. Many of them don't stay where they were put. Ice or storms or even passing ships move them. Sometimes they have to be moved when a channel's course changes because of new dredging.

There are 16,000 aids to navigation that stay fixed in place—the lights and targets that serve for daytime beacons. All show up better in color photographs than in black and white.

UP-TO-DATE CHARTS

The Coast and Geodetic Survey publishes 820 charts, of many types, at many different scales, covering all 12,383 miles of United States coastline. Of these charts, 670 are on a scale so large that the side of this page measures about five nautical miles. A nautical mile equals 6,080 feet.

Every year the Coast and Geodetic Survey issues about twenty new and reconstructed charts, and over 500 revised and reprinted. Even a newly printed chart will be corrected by hand when anything changes, so that no inaccurate information should ever reach a chart buyer. As soon as any chart has been hand-corrected forty times, it will be newly printed. Half the charts reach that point at least once a year.

Hurricane Carla caused a great many revisions in the Galveston chart. It took many months for the Army Engineers, the Coast Guard, and the Coast and Geodetic Survey to compile the changes.

The U.S. Naval Oceanographic Office publishes about 6,000 different charts. They cover the navigable waters of the world away from the United States and its possessions.

Some of Canada's coastline never has been charted, for it is hard to find a coastline which is hidden by ice much of the year. Every year the Canadian government finishes new nautical charts in the far north.

AIDS TO NAVIGATION

When ships are out of sight of land, they face the age-old problem of knowing where they are. Navigators still use dead reckoning—keeping track of how long they go in a certain direction and at what speed. They estimate where they must be. Waves, currents, and wind may alter the course. So they check their position at intervals. The oldest method is still in use. It depends on the guideposts in the sky—sun and stars, accurate tables, and correct time, with the result located on an

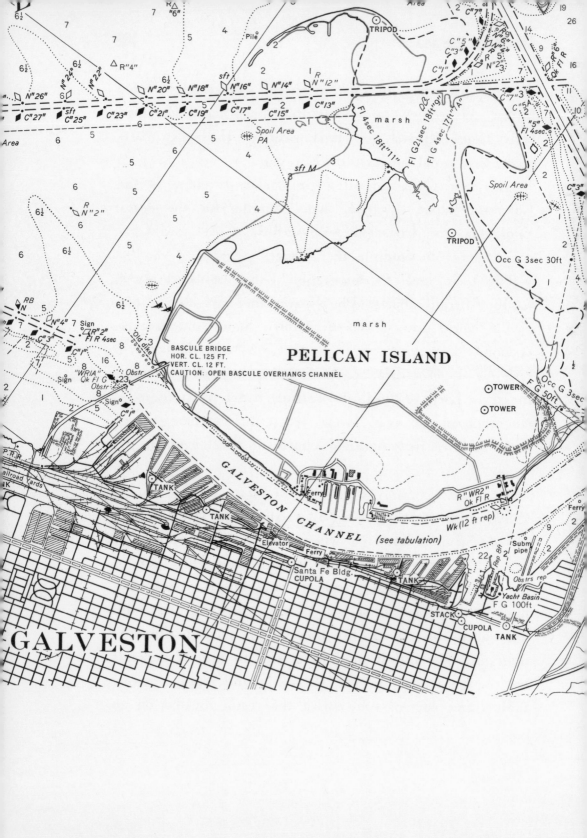

accurate chart.

Two newer methods use radio aids to navigation. They work in fog and darkness and daylight. There must be special charts with curving lines, and the lines for both systems are often on the same chart. There are not yet enough broadcasting stations of this special kind to cover the earth.

The newest method of navigation depends on the Transit satellites. Every twelve hours, ground tracking stations will transmit the satellite's orbit to it. The satellite will store and transmit the information to specially equipped ships at two-minute intervals. It will also broadcast a continuous signal and give the correct time on longitude zero, at Greenwich. The navigator can compute his position in about fifteen minutes with pencil and paper—or almost instantly with a computer. He will still need to locate that position on an accurate chart to know where he is.

There is a new kind of navigator for whom the Coast and Geodetic Survey is making a new series of charts. The skipper who pulls his small boat behind the family automobile until he reaches the water can buy charts in handy spiral-notebook form. The fold-out

Nautical charts had to be brought up to date to show the changes caused near Galveston by Hurricane Carla. Here the older shoreline is shown in blue.

charts are easy to handle, and list other information small boats need such as services and supplies at various harbors. There are even photographs of some of the lighthouses.

Charts
for the Air

When planes were new, they flew so low and so slowly that a pilot could follow roads or railroad tracks from one town to another. Any map helped, if it showed landmarks on the ground.

But today air charts must have special information. In 1923 the Army published the first U.S. air chart, and in 1927 civilian pilots got their first chart. Now in the United States there are over 350,000 civilian pilots, from students to airline transport pilots. For them the U.S. Coast and Geodetic Survey annually produces

40,000,000 copies of 1,500 different aeronautical charts.

Like land maps and nautical charts, air charts are tailored to fit different needs. The owner of a small private plane would not buy the same chart as a jet pilot.

There are two main kinds of charts. One is for pilots who need to see where they are going. They want a chart that looks like the ground below. The other kind is for the pilot whose dashboard is crowded with complicated instruments. This pilot may travel so fast that what he sees ahead of him is already behind him before its existence sinks into his brain.

CHARTS FOR VISUAL FLYING

Even the charts which don't look a bit like a map of the ground are firmly based on the road-map maker's chief source—the quad map. Like the road-map maker, the air-chart maker starts with many quad maps. But some things have to be added. Quad maps aren't revised and reissued as often as air charts must be. So the air-chart maker, studying the latest aerial photographs with a magnifying glass, corrects the quad map by hand.

The chartmaker works with many quad maps to cover the area for one visual air chart. He collects other kinds of facts, too. For a new chart of the section around Washington, D.C., one chartmaker had to

Bringing a quad map up to date by comparing it with the most recent aerial photographs.

consult 1,500 items just to prepare the base map—before adding information useful to planes only.

Then, by a process similar to making road maps, the many quad maps are condensed into the background for an air chart. The Coast and Geodetic Survey charts the

United States and its possessions for planes. For military pilots, the Air Force's Aeronautical Chart and Information Center (ACIC) produces air charts of the rest of the world. Approximately 95,000,000 copies of charts and related items are distributed each year by ACIC.

Some parts of the world do not have as detailed maps as Europe and North America have. Then the chartmaker uses the best maps he can find, and relies more heavily on air photographs. At night or through clouds, pictures can be taken by other methods, such as radar.

The basic part of an air chart for visual flying emphasizes the changing heights. Every thousand feet higher, the color changes. At sea level it is pale green. At a thousand feet it becomes still paler, then a light tan, then various deeper shades.

A pilot could look at an air chart to estimate how long a runway he would need. Air gets thinner at high altitudes. If all other factors are the same, a propeller plane that needs a runway of 7,200 feet at an airport 6,000 feet above sea level would need only a 4,800-foot runway at sea level. A jet that needs 7,100 feet at sea level must have 11,100 feet—more than two miles—to take off at an elevation of 6,000 feet.

The pilot finds his flying height above sea level from his altimeter. He finds the height above sea level of the land below him from his chart. Subtracting gives him the amount of air between him and the ground. A 5,000-foot reading on the altimeter is safe in much of the United States. But at Cheyenne, Santa Fe, or Denver, it would put the pilot underground.

One way of thinking about maps divides the information into natural features (such as rivers) and man-made features (such as roads). On air charts a more useful division is between visible facts and invisible facts.

Many invisible facts need to be on an air chart. Planes usually follow Federal Airways, which are direct routes about ten miles wide. Lines on the chart show the center of the airway, or in some cases its whole width.

Some marks on an air chart—like some road signs along a highway—warn of dangers. A plane must never fly over certain places on the ground, and over others only with advance notice to a Flight Service Station of the Federal Aviation Agency.

A pilot must avoid a high chimney or radio or TV tower. Aviation charts emphasize them with a special symbol. A specialist keeps track of such obstructions and makes sure that they appear on the proper air charts.

Most prominent of all the invisible facts on an air chart are the symbols relating to radio. A pilot can follow radio beams from one airport to another. There

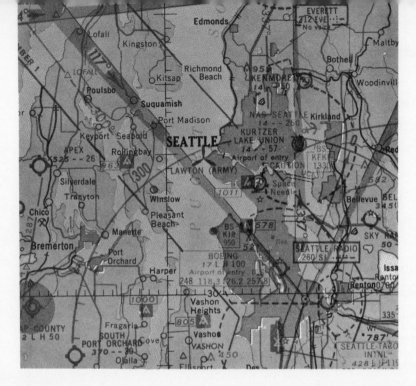

This visual air chart of Seattle warns pilots about the Space Needle built for the World's Fair of 1962. A long arrow points to zero degrees—the direction of magnetic north from Seattle.

are special radio stations for pilots. But even ordinary broadcasting stations help a pilot. Their call letters and frequency appear on charts for low-flying planes.

A big compass-like circle surrounds each station. The compass is tipped so that it shows north just as a real compass would at that place.

For landing and take-off there are special charts on a very large scale. Eighty-seven sectional charts cover the United States. A faster plane might use a World Aeronautical Chart. At a scale of one to a million, it takes 43 of these charts to cover the U.S. The ACIC publishes similar Operational Navigation Charts, with 938 charts covering the land areas of the world. There are also visual air charts, at smaller scales, for larger areas.

CHARTS FOR FLYING BY INSTRUMENT

By the time a pilot is going fast enough to need a small-scale chart, he needs more information for his instruments than for his eyes. In fact, the invisible crowds the visible right off the map. A completely different series of air charts looks as if someone had

Index map of Operational Navigation Charts for Europe, Africa, and part of Asia.

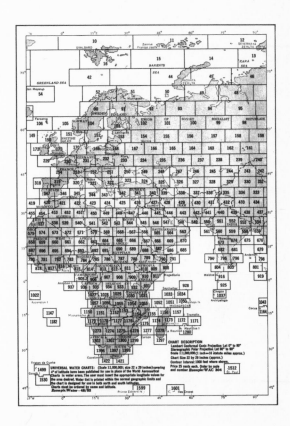

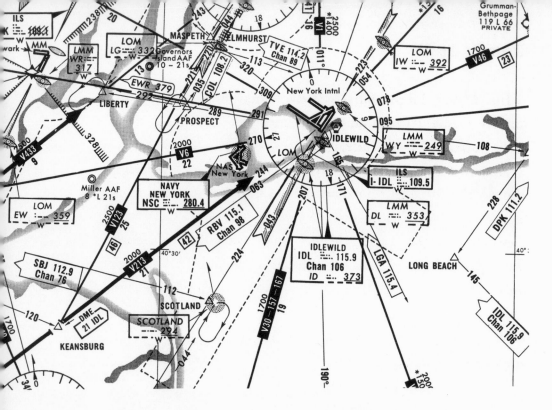

Chart showing New York harbor for low-altitude instrument flying. One inch stands for 7 miles.

printed only the aeronautical overprint and had forgotten to use a base map of the ground.

This series is seven times as popular as the charts for visual flying, and many of the charts come out in a new edition every four weeks. But no ordinary map reader can understand such a chart. He needs to have his mind stocked, as a pilot's is, with all sorts of information about radio navigation. Would you guess that the chart above includes the same area as the nautical chart of the approach to New York harbor on page 95?

Instrument Flight Charts are divided into three types, for low, intermediate, and high altitude. The New York chart is for low altitude.

A new type of chart is for intermediate altitudes, above 14,000 feet but below 24,000. It omits many facts found on low-altitude charts. Even the busy Detroit-Cleveland area seems less crowded because the ordinary broadcasting stations are omitted. Although only the shape of the lakes shows that ground and

Chart showing the Detroit-Cleveland area for intermediate-altitude instrument flying. One inch stands for 32 miles.

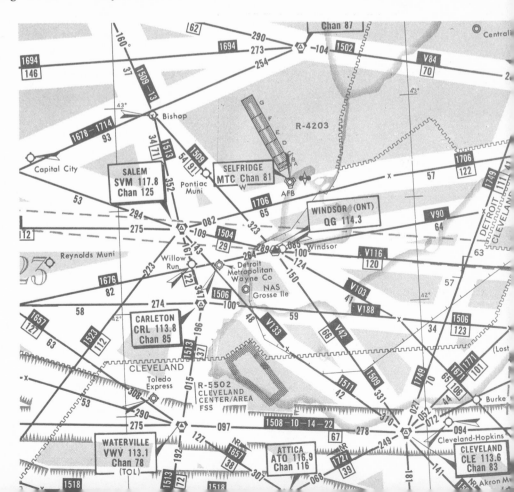

water are below the plane, all the airways and radio
facilities are firmly tied into place as they would be on
a detailed ground map.

Another group of mapmakers produces charts for flying by instrument—Jeppesen and Company. They sell
yearly subscriptions, including frequent revisions, of airway manuals containing air charts and other information
that pilots need. All pilots of all scheduled airlines in
the United States, and many foreign ones, use their
manuals. So do U.S. Army and Navy pilots, wherever
stationed. Special Air Force manuals for flying within
the U.S. are produced under contract.

Maps
for Buried Treasure

MAPS WORTH MILLIONS STOLEN, a newspaper headline may say.

Probably no one would steal an air chart or a road map or even the all-important quad map. It's easy and cheap to buy another copy.

A map that makes headlines is one-of-a-kind—usually a secret guide to buried treasure. It shows invisible facts that only a highly trained man with expensive equipment could locate. Most often a stolen map reveals where there might be oil. It was probably made by private mapmakers for an oil company.

Oil companies build up complete files of underground maps for their territory. All employees who handle the maps are specially insured. One large company estimates that it spent about twelve to fifteen cents a square mile to build up its map library.

It would cost more than that except for the help of government maps. The same organization that makes the basic quad maps—the U.S. Geological Survey—also makes some underground maps. Oil companies can adapt the government maps for their own use. But in many cases no government underground map exists, or the maps are not detailed enough for the oil company, or they show too much information of no interest to the company.

Most underground maps show guesses, because no one can examine what's underfoot at every step. The guesses usually turn out to be facts, because well-trained scientists had good reasons for their guesses.

Geology adds another set of invisible facts to mapmaking. Geologists can discover—and maps can show—the type of soil or rock below the surface, and how the layers fit on top of each other. To obtain this information, men use their eyes, ears, and brains as well as instruments and photographs.

The quickest way to get an idea of the general structure of the surface is from aerial photographs, either in color or in black and white. What shows in the pictures often reveals what is underneath—or what could not be there.

Planes can collect underground facts with special instruments. Geiger counters help find uranium. A "bird" in the plane's tail can record the magnetism of the ground below. It locates iron ore and metals which often occur with iron, such as copper, lead, nickel, asbestos, sulphur, gold, titanium, and chromium. The bird is a powerful magnet, called a *magnetometer*. Planes formerly pulled birds far below the plane to avoid the magnetic attraction of the plane itself. Now special magnets inside the plane neutralize each other. Some companies also use a bird to help find places where there might be oil.

A graph in the magnetometer records the magnetic pull as the plane flies back and forth. Then a mapmaker uses the graph to make a special underground map. The surface of the ground shows just enough to help the map user get to places where the magnetism is most intense. The magnetic pull between earth and plane is strongest at the X. The map on the next page shows a different use of contour lines: to represent magnetic pull instead of height.

Sound can measure distance under ground, as well as under water. The sound of an explosion travels through different kinds of material at different rates. When it reaches bedrock, it sends back an echo. Explosions at different places can show the shape of an underground structure. Oil companies use these man-made earthquakes to find pockets likely to contain oil.

There's no substitute for a trained man at finding what is below ground. He can look at the layers of rock as they show in a canyon, notice the way they tilt, and predict where the layers will come to the sur-face again. He can study the layers in a mine shaft, or in a long core bored from the earth. He can chip off

Here contour lines are used to show strength of magnetic pull. The pull is strong-est at point X.

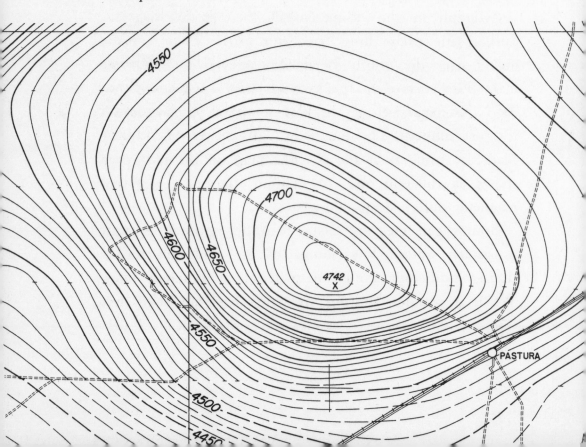

A draftsman prepares a cross-section for an underground map.

pieces and put them through all kinds of tests in a laboratory.

An underground map may contain so much information that mapmakers have to be ingenious to find ways to show it all. Some underground maps are beautiful. The base map is a quad map. Transparent color added to the map shows what material is below ground. A draftsman can also use patterns of dots and stripes for additional information.

To show how the layers fit on top of each other, a cross-section drawing is placed along the edge of the map. It looks like the side of an excavation for a building—with the earth sliced open.

Mapmaking
Around the World

Good mapmakers all over the world try to make accurate, readable maps, especially of their own lands. Europeans, who claim to be more map-conscious than Americans, have mapped their countries very thoroughly. U.S. mapmakers admire maps made in Sweden and Switzerland and Russia and Great Britain.

In 1959 a Danish mapmaker compiled the first map of all western Europe based on a unified system of survey markers. Until then the maps made in one country wouldn't fit smoothly with maps made in another country. For it was not until 1951 that an international team of surveyors began to adjust the basic ground markers all over Europe to one another.

Mapmakers and map users want the best map of an area, no matter who made it. For many generations sailors from all countries used England's nautical charts. Mapmakers buy each others products. More copies of France's collection of maps, or Atlas, have been sold outside France than in France itself. Large libraries have maps in Chinese, German, and many other languages.

Countries with highly skilled mapmakers are helping other countries all over the world in all phases of mapping. For example, the U.S. Coast and Geodetic Survey sent twelve men to help 59 Ethiopians establish the first accurate framework of ground markers in that country. It took four years, and covered about a fourth of the country. Now it is possible for the Ethiopian government to plan flood control and irrigation.

In South America, 17 nations are working with United States mapmakers to continue the system of ground markers which now ties all of North America together. It will be the longest continuous framework in the world.

A new system of navigation, called Radan, is so accurate that a plane can find its way over trackless jungle or desert even without any radio signals for guidance. In this way, aerial exploration for minerals and oil can be carried out more cheaply and quickly than ever before.

Intensive world-wide mapping can penetrate thick jungles to find land suitable for farming. Mapmakers are discovering not only new resources but islands and mountains previously unknown. They are taking some places off the map, too. At least five islands in the Arctic have turned out to be imaginary—an earlier mapmaker's interpretation of thick fog or ice.

For nearly a hundred years, mapmakers have held a series of International Congresses. They have shared new and better methods and agreed on ways to make mapping more uniform. They agreed to use Greenwich as the zero meridian, to divide the world into time zones, and to use the simplified measurement provided by the metric system. (Mapmakers of English-speaking nations haven't yet switched from inches, feet, yards, and miles—although most of their scientists have.)

The United Nations is now the clearing house for the International Map of the World. This is a collection of maps which mapmakers started to plan in 1891. Each country is supposed to map its country in the same way, so that all the maps will fit together. The maps are at a scale of one to a million—about 16 miles to one inch. They all use the same symbols, and they are printed in several languages. All the land areas in the world are covered by these maps except for the

tip of Africa and part of the United States and most of
Canada. In these countries there are air charts on the
same scale, but these will have to be adapted to meet
the requirements of the International Map of the World.

The U.S. Army Map Service is helping some nations
in South America and in Asia to map their territory on
a much larger scale—one to 50,000, or less than a
mile to an inch. Each map is printed both in English
and in the language of the country. About 500 different
maps a year have been made recently to help in planning economic development of the countries.

*Part of U.S. Army Map Service map of Saigon and surrounding territory in Viet-
nam. The scale is 1 to 1,000,000—about 16 miles to the inch.*

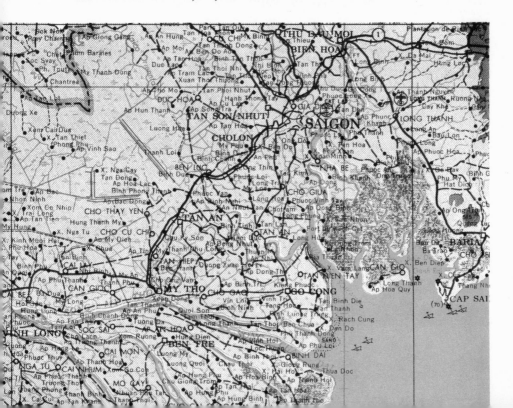

By agreement, certain countries save time and money by reproducing each other's charts and maps with slight alterations. The United States has agreements with Canada, Germany, the Philippines, and Brazil for the exchange of nautical charts.

The Army Map Service must be prepared to furnish large quantities of maps of any part of the world on short notice. Using a conventional printing press, it is just as expensive to print a few copies of a map as it would be to print thousands, and it takes a long time to get the press ready. So, until recently, large quantities of maps had to be printed and stored for possible use. The maps were soon out of date and had to be replaced.

Late in 1963 the system changed, after ten years of work by the U.S. Corps of Engineers Research and Development Agency, at Fort Belvoir, Virginia. Now the map information can be stored on microfilms smaller than a page of this book. The enlarged maps can be printed when needed, in as many as five different colors, at the rate of 2,000 an hour. The new electrostatic printing machine is lightweight and could fit on a big truck.

Mapping
the Moon and Sun

There's a new objective for maps and charts—the moon. Several U.S. government agencies are mapping the moon—the Geological Survey, the Army Map Service, and the Air Force's Aeronautical Chart and Information Center.

Lunar maps and charts show many of the same features as quad maps: lines of latitude and longitude, as well as contour lines and shaded relief for heights.

The ACIC released its first lunar chart to the public in July, 1961. The Air Force got it a year earlier. By early 1963, six other moon charts were ready.

All air charts, including those of the moon, carry a printed request that the user correct the chart when he discovers mistakes, and send it back to the ACIC. In return the astronomer—or, later, the astronaut—will get a free replacement copy.

Index map of the ACIC's lunar charts, showing numbers assigned to the side of the moon we can see. Other numbers will be used someday for charts of the moon's far side. These charts are on the same scale as the ACIC's Operational Navigational Charts illustrated on page 111.

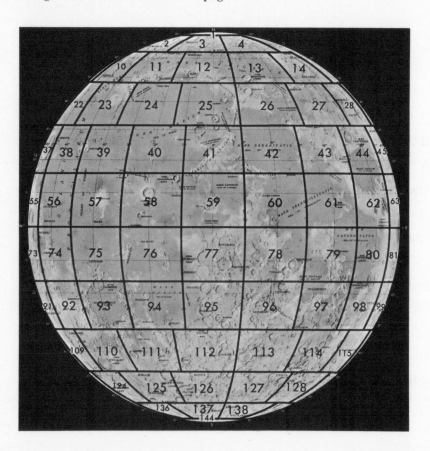

PHOTOGRAPHS FOR LUNAR MAPS

Up to now, all lunar mapmaking has been done from the earth. Skilled astronomers help mapmakers to interpret photographs taken by many different observatories. They also study the moon through telescopes because the human eye can see more than the best camera can. For heights, the ACIC uses a method of comparing how shadows of a ridge or crater vary at different times.

The U.S. Air Force has issued three collections of pictures which show large-scale photographs of all sections of the visible side of the moon. The first atlas contains 280 of the best available photographs from many different observatories. There are four pictures of each moon section, for the sun's rays at different angles can make a feature either very prominent or almost invisible.

Another atlas turned selected pictures into photo maps by printing over the pictures a gridwork of mapmaker's lines of position.

The latest atlas contains photographs that have been projected on a curved surface to simulate the moon and then rephotographed.

The Army Map Service is making large-scale topographic maps of the moon. The mapmakers use two pictures to get a stereo effect, just as the makers of the basic quad maps of the United States do. Stereo photography was first used for moon mapping in 1960.

To get usable stereo picture pairs of the faraway moon, the pictures should be taken from places at least 60,000 miles apart. But places on opposite sides of the earth at the equator are less than 8,000 miles apart.

Fortunately, time can substitute for distance. Even though the moon keeps the same face generally toward the earth, it tips slightly in various directions. Sometimes we can see a little farther around in one way, then a little farther in another. So photographs taken at different times may look as if they had been taken at the same time by two satellites—one 30,000 miles from the earth's center in one direction, the other 30,000 miles away in another direction.

After studying a great many photographs of the moon, the Army Map Service found that some photographs taken by the Paris Observatory between 1896 and 1907 were best for stereo use.

Until we have a space ship orbiting the moon, there will be special problems for lunar mapmakers. The Russians have published photographs of part of the far side, but mapmakers want more and better ones.

Pictures taken from the earth of the side facing us must be greatly enlarged. The Army Map Service uses closed-circuit television and zoom lenses. The moon is small enough to make its surface steeply curved. So mapmakers use a curved tracing table to re-produce the moon's curve.

A highly accurate earth map, as we have seen, starts from basic measurements—ground markers for distance and direction, and bench marks for height above sea level. Because the moon has no sea, the point which appeared to be lowest was chosen to be the zero point. Any lower spots which may be discovered later will be labeled with a minus sign.

As a temporary substitute for ground markers, lunar mapmakers use control points which astronomers have located on moon photographs. About 150 points have been carefully measured as to their relative heights, and their distance and direction from each other.

There are large-scale Army maps of the east and west halves and of the center of the moon's visible face. They all come in three editions—with contour lines; with tints emphasizing certain contour lines; or with colorful shaded relief added.

The visible surface of the moon covers about nine million square miles. This is equivalent to the area covered by North America.

On the moon, as well as on the earth, men may soon try to find underground treasures. The Geological Survey is preparing maps showing what astronomers have learned so far about the surface of the moon, and what geologists believe may lie below the surface. Unmanned moon probes will send back radio and television information about the moon's surface. There will be close-up pictures, and data about gravity, magnetism, and the kinds of elements detected. Perhaps there will be evidence of moonquakes.

Now mapmakers are using stereo pictures to make geologic moon maps. Mirrors reflect the two pictures so the compiler sees them as one three-dimensional picture. She must interpret what she sees, just as if she were making a map of what is underground on earth. She draws a geologic map, showing the relative ages of the formations composing the moon's surface and the folds and fractures in it.

A Geological Survey map compiler works from stereo photographs of the moon.

Another kind of map is called a physiographic map. This one uses a photographic map as a base. The mapmaker adds names and outlines of regions on the moon—highlands, lowlands, dry seas, and smaller subdivisions. Important sharp ridges are emphasized with red lines.

MAPPING THE SUN

The sun is being mapped, too. But it's a more difficult subject because it changes constantly in appearance. During the International Geophysical Year, stations around the earth took daily photographs. Now those pictures are being transformed into maps of the sun and its corona.

The same study will continue during the International Year of the Quiet Sun—as it will indefinitely. During a solar flare, pictures are taken every ten or fifteen seconds so that a map can be compiled of the life history of that particular flare.

From Map
to Mind

What makes a good map? Accuracy, first of all. But, unless the reader understands the map, it is useless to him.

A well-drawn map can show many more facts in the same space—and yet appear less crowded—than a poorly drawn map. The U.S. Geological Survey is making experimental maps, trying to arrange lines, colors, and type so that an average map reader will notice the most important features first. For tests have revealed that most people notice colors in a certain order, and that smaller type of some styles can be read more

With an airbrush, Hal Shelton portrays shaded relief for a map of Utah.

easily than larger letters of other type faces.

One kind of map that is particularly easy to understand looks something like a color photograph taken from an orbiting satellite. An international meeting of mapmakers awarded prizes to Hal Shelton, the inventor of that type of map. His very accurate and detailed maps are like color photographs taken in summer, because deserts are sand-colored, while forests, swamps, and grasslands are various shades of green. He uses an airbrush to draw the shadows of hills as he colors them so it is easy to see the higher ground. Very high mountains are white, for they are usually snow-covered.

The Army Map Service discovered that very few people know how to read contour lines skillfully. So it developed another way to show hills on maps. The hills rise up above the surface of the map, just as real hills rise up above surrounding ground.

Museums frequently have that type of map, which is called a raised-relief map. The mapmaker builds a clay model of the land, and the map reader can feel as well as see the hills.

The Army Map Service developed an inexpensive way to make large quantities of raised-relief maps quickly. They start with a clay model, made over layers cut to represent the contour lines on a quad map. The map itself is printed on flat plastic sheets. At just the right temperature, in a heating box, the plastic softens, and the printed map fits down into every indentation in the clay model.

Civilians can buy the same type of map from the Aero Service Corporation. There are world maps, maps of continents, a map of Canada, of the United States, some separate states, and a series based on Geological Survey quad maps. The same company does much aerial exploration and mapping both here and abroad. It took one set of photographs for the Rifle quad map.

Removing a raised-relief map from the heating box.

Some maps, printed in fluorescent ink, can be read under ultra-violet light. This means that a navigator at sea or in the air can keep his eyes adjusted to darkness.

Many countries publish national collections of maps called Atlases. The United States is producing a National Atlas—about 400 pages of general reference maps and special subject maps. Selected sheets (4 pages each) may be sold, as they are published, through the Map Distribution Branch of the Geological Survey. A revision program provides for keeping the maps current and issuing new editions of the Atlas.

Every ten years, after the census, there will be new
U.S. maps showing the new population distribution. New
boundaries will show new election districts.

Satellites revealed that magnetic fields around the
earth trap and channel high energy particles—the Van
Allen radiation belts. They have been mapped both before and after an atomic test disturbed their pattern.

Mapmakers are doing more and more of the brain-
work for the map reader. Some even make maps that
tell a person where he is on the map. New electronic
maps for pilots combine a map, a computer, and a
projection screen. As a plane 50,000 feet above the
earth flies at 1500 miles an hour, it won't matter
whether clouds obscure the earth. The part of the map
which represents the ground below will be projected
onto a screen. A cross will show the pilot the
exact spot on the map which is below the plane.

Colonel John Glenn, first U.S. astronaut to orbit the
earth, had a similar device. It is a small globe which
can revolve slowly, duplicating the position of the real
earth beneath the astronaut's spacecraft.

After an astronaut reaches orbit, ground stations tell
him where he is. He can set the bull's-eye in the
globe's window to point to the ground below. Then he
can set the controls so that as he moves over the earth,
the little globe turns and keeps the bull's-eye always

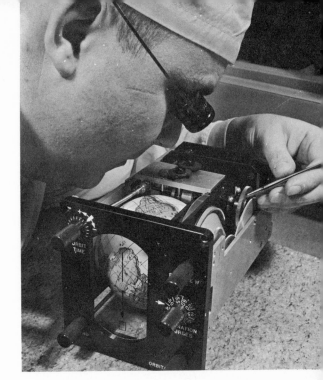

Looking through the window of this instrument, an orbiting astronaut could tell not only his current position, but where he would land if he returned immediately to earth.

in correct position. The arrow points to the part of the globe where he would land if he fired the retro-rockets to return himself to earth.

For most people no one is going to spend a fortune to provide a self-reading map. Mapmakers will keep on producing accurate, readable, inexpensive maps. The map reader will have to use his own computer inside his head to figure out what kind of map he needs, where to get it, and how to use it.

How to Find
the Maps You Want

In person

Public library
Tourist bureau
Filling station (for road maps)
Map dealers
   Map stores (listed under "Maps" in classified telephone book)
   Bookstores and stationery stores
   Nautical supply stores (at seaports)
   Aeronautical supply stores (at airports)

By mail

*Each of the following organizations will send you, on request, a catalog
or index map with a price list.*

U.S. topographic quadrangle maps and National Atlas Sheets	
East of the Mississippi	U.S. Geological Survey Washington 25, D.C.
West of the Mississippi	U.S. Geological Survey Denver Federal Center Denver 25, Colorado
U.S. nautical charts and aeronautical charts	U.S. Coast and Geodetic Survey Washington 25, D.C.
Other U.S. maps	Division of Public Documents Government Printing Office Washington 25, D.C.
Canadian topographic maps, aircharts, and nautical charts	Surveys and Mapping Branch Department of Mines and Technical Surveys 615 Booth Street Ottawa, Canada
Maps of other countries	U.S. Army Map Service Washington 25, D.C.
Foreign nautical charts	U.S. Naval Oceanographic Office Washington 25, D.C.

Foreign aeronautical charts

Aeronautical Chart and Information
  Center
U.S. Air Force
Second and Arsenal
St. Louis 18, Missouri

Maps of the moon

U.S. Air Force Lunar Charts
Superintendent of Documents
U.S. Government Printing Office
Washington 25, D.C.

Geologic Moon Maps
U.S. Geological Survey
Washington 25, D.C.

U.S. Army Map Service
Washington 25, D.C.

Sky Publishing Corporation
49M Bay State Road
Cambridge 38, Massachusetts

For help in locating any map published by a U.S. government agency or by a private company, write to

Map Information Office
U.S. Geological Survey
Washington 25, D.C.

Index

About the author

Susan Marsh is an enthusiastic user of maps—charts for sailing
Long Island Sound, contour maps for climbing Colorado's high
Rockies, and road maps for extensive trips with her husband
and their four children. She has written many articles for the
New York Times, including "You Can Watch Your Government
Making Maps."

A Smith College graduate, Mrs. Marsh is licensed as a substitute teacher in the Denver schools. She also plays the viola in
the Denver Symphony.